Plastic
TOY CARS
of the 1950s & 1960s

The Collector's Guide

C000108812

More from Veloce Publishing –

SpeedPro Series
4-Cylinder Engine – How to Blueprint & Build a Short Block for High Performance (Hammill)
Alfa Romeo DOHC High-Performance Manual (Kartalamakis)
Alfa Romeo V6 Engine High-Perfomance Manual (Kartalamakis)
BMC 998cc A-Series Engine – How to Power Tune (Hammill)
1275cc A-Series High-Performance Manual (Hammill)
Camshafts – How to Choose & Time them for Maximum Power (Hammill)
Cylinder Heads – How to Build, Modify & Power Tune Updated & Revised Edition (Burgess & Gollan)
Distributor-type Ignition Systems – How to Build & Power Tune (Hammill)
Fast Road Car – How to Plan and Build Revised & Updated Colour New Edition (Stapleton)
Ford SOHC 'Pinto' & Sierra Cosworth DOHC Engines – How to Power Tune Updated & Enlarged Edition (Hammill)
Ford V8 – How to Power Tune Small Block Engines (Hammill)
Harley-Davidson Evolution Engines – How to Build & Power Tune (Hammill)
Holley Carburetors – How to Build & Power Tune Revised & Updated Edition (Hammill)
Jaguar XK Engines – How to Power Tune Revised & Updated Colour Edition (Hammill)
MG Midget & Austin-Healey Sprite – How to Power Tune Updated & Revised Edition (Stapleton)
MGB 4-Cylinder Engine – How to Power Tune (Burgess)
MGB V8 Power – How to Give Your, Third Colour Edition (Williams)
MGB, MGC & MGB V8 – How to Improve (Williams)
Mini Engines – How to Power Tune on a Small Budget Colour Edition (Hammill)
Motorcycle-engined Racing Car – How to Build (Pashley)
Motorsport – Getting Started (Collins)
Motorsports Datalogging (Templeman)
Nitrous Oxide High-Performance Manual (Langfield)
Rover V8 Engines – How to Power Tune (Hammill)
Sportscar/Kitcar Suspension & Brakes – How to Build & Modify Enlarged & Updated 2nd Edition (Hammill)
SU Carburettor High-Performance Manual (Hammill)
Supercar, How to Build (Thompson)
Suzuki 4x4 – How to Modify for Serious Off-Road Action (Richardson)
Tiger Avon Sportscar – How to Build Your Own Updated & Revised 2nd Edition (Dudley)
TR2, 3 & TR4 – How to Improve (Williams)
TR5, 250 & TR6 – How to Improve (Williams)
TR7 & TR8, How to Improve (Williams)
V8 Engine – How to Build a Short Block for High Performance (Hammill)
Volkswagen Beetle Suspension, Brakes & Chassis – How to Modify for High Performance (Hale)
Volkswagen Bus Suspension, Brakes & Chassis – How to Modify for High Performance (Hale)
Weber DCOE, & Dellorto DHLA Carburetors – How to Build & Power Tune 3rd Edition (Hammill)

Those were the days ... Series
Alpine Trials & Rallies 1910-1973 (Pfundner)
Austerity Motoring (Bobbitt)
Brighton National Speed Trials (Gardiner)
British Police Cars (Walker)
British Woodies (Peck)
Crystal Palace by (Collins)
Dune Buggy Phenomenon (Hale)
Dune Buggy Phenomenon Volume 2 (Hale)
MG's Abingdon Factory (Moylan)
Motor Racing at Brands Hatch in the Seventies (Parker)
Motor Racing at Goodwood in the Sixties (Gardiner)
Motor Racing at Oulton Park in the 1960s (McFadyen)
Motor Racing at Oulton Park in the 1970s (McFadyen)
Short Oval Racing in the 1980s (Neil)
Three Wheelers (Bobbitt)

Enthusiast's Restoration Manual Series
Citroën 2CV, How to Restore (Porter)
Classic Car Bodywork, How to Restore (Thaddeus)
Classic Car Electrics (Thaddeus)
Classic Cars, How to Paint (Thaddeus)
Reliant Regal, How to Restore (Payne)
Triumph TR2/3/3A, How to Restore (Williams)
Triumph TR4/4A, How to Restore (Williams)
Triumph TR5/250 & 6, How to Restore (Williams)
Triumph TR7/8, How to Restore (Williams)
Volkswagen Beetle, How to Restore (Tyler)
VW Bay Window Bus (Paxton)
Yamaha FS1-E, How to Restore (Watts)

Essential Buyer's Guide Series
Alfa GT (Booker)
Alfa Romeo Spider Giulia (Booker)
BMW GS (Henshaw)
BSA Bantam (Henshaw)
BSA Twins (Henshaw)
Citroën 2CV (Paxton)
Citroën ID & DS (Heilig)
Fiat 500 & 600 (Bobbitt)
Jaguar E-type 3.8 & 4.2-litre (Crespin)
Jaguar E-type V12 5.3-litre (Crespin)
Jaguar/Daimler XJ6, XJ12 & Sovereign (Crespin)
Jaguar XJ-S (Crespin)
MGB & MGB GT (Williams)
Mercedes-Benz 280SL-560SL Roadsters (Bass)
Mercedes-Benz 'Pagoda' 230SL, 250SL & 280SL Roadsters & Coupés (Bass)
Morris Minor (Newell)
Porsche 928 (Hemmings)
Rolls-Royce Silver Shadow & Bentley T-Series (Bobbitt)
Subaru Impreza (Hobbs)
Triumph Bonneville (Henshaw)
Triumph TR6 (Williams)
VW Beetle (Cservenka & Copping)
VW Bus (Cservenka & Copping)

Auto-Graphics Series
Fiat-based Abarths (Sparrow)
Jaguar MkI & II Saloons (Sparrow)
Lambretta LI series scooters (Sparrow)

Rally Giants Series
Audi Quattro (Robson)
Big Healey – 100-Six & 3000 (Robson)
Ford Escort MkI (Robson)
Ford Escort RS1800 (Robson)
Lancia Stratos (Robson)
Peugeot 205 T16 (Robson)
Subaru Impreza (Robson)

General
1½-litre GP Racing 1961-1965 (Whitelock)
AC Two-litre Saloons & Buckland Sportscars (Archibald)
According to Carter (Skelton)
Alfa Romeo Giulia Coupé GT & GTA (Tipler)
Alfa Romeo Montreal - The Essential Companion (Taylor)
Alfa Tipo 33 (McDonough & Collins)
Anatomy of the Works Minis (Moylan)
Armstrong-Siddeley (Smith)
Autodrome (Collins & Ireland)
Automotive A-Z, Lane's Dictionary of Automotive Terms (Lane)
Automotive Mascots (Kay & Springate)
Bahamas Speed Weeks, The (O'Neil)
Bentley Continental, Corniche and Azure (Bennett)
Bentley MkVI, Rolls-Royce Silver Wraith, Dawn & Cloud/Bentley R & S-series (Nutland)
BMC Competitions Department Secrets (Turner, Chambers Browning)
BMW 5-Series (Cranswick)
BMW Z-Cars (Taylor)
British 250cc Racing Motorcycles by Chris Pereira
British Cars, The Complete Catalogue of, 1895-1975 (Culshaw & Horrobin)
BRM – a mechanic's tale (Salmon)
BRM V16 (Ludvigsen)
BSA Bantam Bible (Henshaw)
Bugatti Type 40 (Price)
Bugatti 46/50 Updated Edition (Price & Arbey)
Bugatti T44 & T49 (Price & Arbey)
Bugatti 57 2nd Edition (Price)
Caravans, The Illustrated History 1919-1959 (Jenkinson)
Caravans, The Illustrated History from 1960 (Jenkinson)
Carrera Panamericana (Tipler)
Chrysler 300 – America's Most Powerful Car 2nd Edition (Ackerson)
Chrysler PT Cruiser (Ackerson)
Citroën DS (Bobbitt)
Cliff Alison - From the Fells to Ferrari (Gauld)
Cobra – The Real Thing! (Legate)
Cortina – Ford's Bestseller (Robson)
Coventry Climax Racing Engines (Hammill)
Daimler SP250 New Edition (Long)
Datsun Fairlady Roadster to 280ZX – The Z-car Story (Long)
Dino – The V6 Ferrari (Long)
Dodge Charger – Enduring Thunder (Ackerson)
Dodge Dynamite! (Grist)
Draw & Paint Cars – How to (Gardiner)
Drive on the Wild Side, A – 20 extreme driving adventures from around the world (Weaver)
Ducati 750 Bible, The (Falloon)
Ducati 860, 900 and Mille Bible, The (Falloon)
Dune Buggy, Building a – The Essential Manual (Shakespeare)
Dune Buggy Files (Hale)
Dune Buggy Handbook (Hale)
Edward Turner: the man behind the motorcycles (Clew)
Fiat & Abarth 124 Spider & Coupé (Tipler)
Fiat & Abarth 500 & 600 2nd edition (Bobbitt)
Fiats, Great Small (Ward)
Fine Art of the Motorcycle Engine, The (Peirce)
Ford F100/F150 Pick-up 1948-1996 (Ackerson)
Ford F150 1997-2005 (Ackerson)
Ford GT – Then, and Now (Streather)
Ford GT40 (Legate)
Ford in Miniature (Olson)
Ford Model Y (Roberts)
Ford Thunderbird from 1954, The Book of the (Long)
Forza Minardi! (Vigar)
Funky Mopeds (Skelton)
Funky Motorcycles (Skelton)
Gentleman Jack (Gauld)
GM in Miniature (Olson)
GT – The World's Best GT Cars 1953-73 (Dawson)
Hillclimbing & sprinting – The essential manual (Short)
Honda NSX (Long)
Jaguar, The Rise of (Price)
Jaguar XJ-S (Long)
Jeep CJ (Ackerson)
Jeep Wrangler (Ackerson)
Karmann-Ghia Coupé & Convertible (Bobbitt)
Lambretta Bible, The (Davies)
Lancia 037 (Collins)
Lancia Delta HF Integrale (Blaettel & Wagner)
Land Rover, The Half-Ton Military (Cook)
Laverda Twins & Triples Bible 1968-1986 (Falloon)
Lea-Francis Story, The (Price)
Lexus Story, The (Long)
little book of smart, The (Jackson)
Lola – The Illustrated History (1957-1977) (Starkey)
Lola – All the Sports Racing & Single-Seater Racing Cars 1978-1997 (Starkey)
Lola T70 – The Racing History & Individual Chassis Record 3rd Edition (Starkey)
Lotus 49 (Oliver)
MarketingMobiles, The Wonderful Wacky World of (Hale)
Mazda MX-5/Miata 1.6 Enthusiast's Workshop Manual (Grainger & Shoemark)
Mazda MX-5/Miata 1.8 Enthusiast's Workshop Manual (Grainger & Shoemark)
Mazda MX-5 Miata: the book of the world's favourite sportscar (Long)
Mazda MX-5 Miata Roadster (Long)
MGA (Price Williams)
MGB & MGB GT – Expert Guide (Auto-Doc Series) (Williams)
MGB Electrical Systems (Astley)
Micro Caravans (Jenkinson)
Micro Trucks (Mort)
Microcars at large! (Quellin)
Mini Cooper – The Real Thing! (Tipler)
Mitsubishi Lancer Evo, the road car & WRC story (Long)
Montlhéry, the story of the Paris autodrome (Boddy)
Morgan Maverick (Lawrence)
Morris Minor, 60 years on the road (Newell)
Moto Guzzi Sport & Le Mans Bible (Falloon)
Motor Movies – The Posters! (Veysey)
Motor Racing – Reflections of a Lost Era (Carter)
Motorcycle Road & Racing Chassis Designs (Knoakes)
Motorhomes, The Illustrated History (Jenkinson)
Motorsport in colour, 1950s (Wainwright)
Nissan 300ZX & 350Z – The Z-Car Story (Long)
Pass the Theory and Practical Driving Tests (Gibson & Hoole)
Peking to Paris 2007 (Young)
Plastic Toy Cars of the 1950s & 1960s (Ralston)
Pontiac Firebird (Cranswick)
Porsche Boxster (Long)
Porsche 356 (2nd edition) (Long)
Porsche 911 Carrera – The Last of the Evolution (Corlett)
Porsche 911R, RS & RSR, 4th Edition (Starkey)
Porsche 911 – The Definitive History 1963-1971 (Long)
Porsche 911 – The Definitive History 1971-1977 (Long)
Porsche 911 – The Definitive History 1977-1987 (Long)
Porsche 911 – The Definitive History 1987-1997 (Long)
Porsche 911 – The Definitive History 1997-2004 (Long)
Porsche 911SC 'Super Carrera' – The Essential Companion (Streather)
Porsche 914 & 914-6: The Definitive History Of The Road & Competition Cars (Long)
Porsche 924 (Long)
Porsche 944 (Long)
Porsche 993 'King of Porsche' – The Essential Companion (Streather)
Porsche 996 'Supreme Porsche' – The Essential Companion (Streather)
Porsche Racing Cars – 1953 to 1975 (Long)
Porsche Racing Cars – 1976 on (Long)
Porsche – The Rally Story (Meredith)
Porsche: Three Generations of Genius (Meredith)
RAC Rally Action! (Gardiner)
Rallye Sport Fords: the inside story (Moreton)
Redman, Jim – 6 Times World Motorcycle Champion: The Autobiography (Redman)
Rolls-Royce Silver Shadow/Bentley T Series Corniche & Camargue Revised & Enlarged Edition (Bobbitt)
Rolls-Royce Silver Spirit, Silver Spur & Bentley Mulsanne 2nd Edition (Bobbitt)
RX-7 – Mazda's Rotary Engine Sportscar (updated & revised new edition) (Long)
Scooters & Microcars, The A-Z of popular (Dan)
Scooter Lifestyle (Grainger)
Singer Story: Cars, Commercial Vehicles, Bicycles & Motorcycles (Atkinson)
SM – Citroën's Maserati-engined Supercar (Long & Claverol)
Subaru Impreza: the road car and WRC story (Long)
Taxi! The Story of the 'London' Taxicab (Bobbitt)
Tinplate Toy Cars of the 1950s & 1960s (Ralston)
Toyota Celica & Supra, The book of Toyota's Sports Coupés (Long)
Toyota MR2 Coupés & Spyders (Long)
Triumph Motorcycles & the Meriden Factory (Hancox)
Triumph Speed Twin & Thunderbird Bible (Woolridge)
Triumph Tiger Cub Bible (Estall)
Triumph Trophy Bible (Woolridge)
Triumph TR6 (Kimberley)
Unraced (Collins)
Velocette Motorcycles – MSS to Thruxton Updated & Revised (Burris)
Virgil Exner – Visioneer: The official biography of Virgil M Exner designer extraordinaire (Grist)
Volkswagen Bus Book, The (Bobbitt)
Volkswagen Bus or Van to Camper, How to Convert (Porter)
Volkswagens of the World (Glen)
VW Beetle Cabriolet (Bobbitt)
VW Beetle – The Car of the 20th Century (Copping)
VW Bus – 40 years of Splitties, Bays & Wedges (Copping)
VW Bus Book, The (Bobbitt)
VW Golf: five generations of fun (Copping & Cservenka)
VW – The air-cooled era (Copping)
VW T5 Camper Conversion Manual (Porter)
VW Campers (Copping)
Works Minis, The Last (Purves & Brenchley)
Works Rally Mechanic (Moylan)

www.velocebooks.com

First published in November 2007 by Veloce Publishing Limited, 33 Trinity Street, Dorchester DT1 1TT, England. Fax 01305 268864/e-mail info@veloce.co.uk/web www.veloce.co.uk or www.velocebooks.com.
ISBN: 978-1-845841-25-6/UPC: 6-36847-04125-0
© Andrew Ralston and Veloce Publishing 2007. All rights reserved. With the exception of quoting brief passages for the purpose of review, no part of this publication may be recorded, reproduced or transmitted by any means, including photocopying, without the written permission of Veloce Publishing Ltd. Throughout this book logos, model names and designations, etc, have been used for the purposes of identification, illustration and decoration. Such names are the property of the trademark holder as this is not an official publication.
Readers with ideas for automotive books, or books on other transport or related hobby subjects, are invited to write to the editorial director of Veloce Publishing at the above address.
British Library Cataloguing in Publication Data - A catalogue record for this book is available from the British Library. Typesetting, design and page make-up all by Veloce Publishing Ltd on Apple Mac.
Printed in India by Replika Press.

Plastic TOY CARS

of the 1950s & 1960s

The Collector's Guide

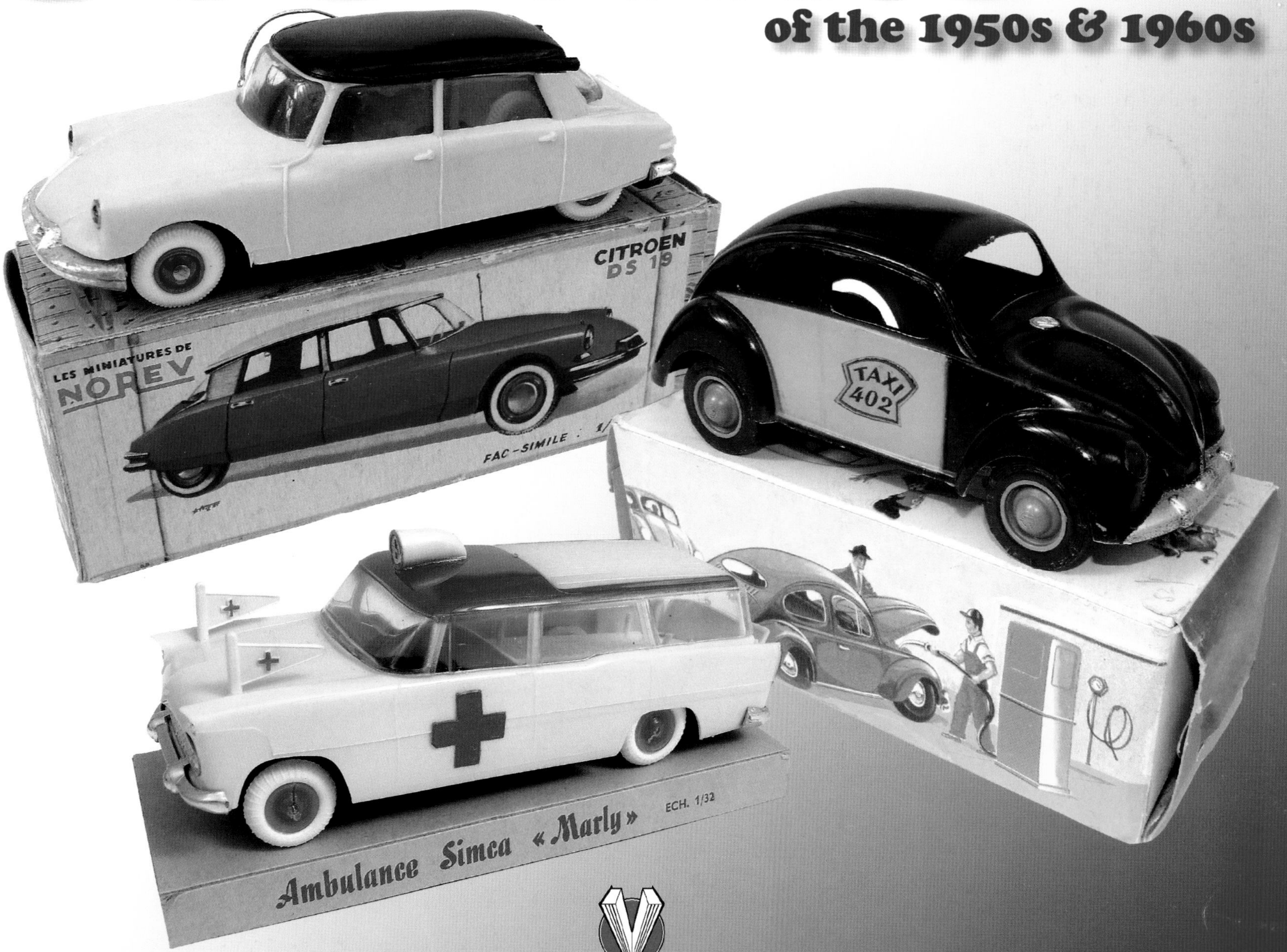

CITROEN DS 19

LES MINIATURES DE NOREV

FAC-SIMILE : 1/

TAXI 402

Ambulance Simca « Marly »   ECH. 1/32

VELOCE PUBLISHING
THE PUBLISHER OF FINE AUTOMOTIVE BOOKS

Andrew Ralston

CONTENTS

**MORAY COUNCIL
LIBRARIES &
INFO.SERVICES**

20 21 97 94

Askews	
629.221075	

FOREWORD

A ndrew Ralston has been a regular contributor of articles to *Diecast Collector* and other magazines for a number of years. As a life-long collector he has a wide knowledge of many different types of model, but one of his specific interests has been the various French ranges. These include Norev and Minialuxe, which both produced model cars with plastic bodies back in the 1950s. It therefore comes as no surprise that Andrew is something of an authority on plastic models.

Over the last 30-40 years, the hobby of collecting models, mainly those with bodies made of diecast metal, has become a pastime enjoyed by many people, the resulting value of the items in their collections being an added incentive. Many manufacturers have capitalised on this interest and produced ranges specifically intended for collectors. This has, in turn, led to the publication of magazines to serve this hobby, including *Diecast Collector*.

Meanwhile, the many toys and models made of plastic over the last 50 years or so have been overlooked by many collectors, which is a shame, as many of them are as well-made and realistic as their metal counterparts and as deserving of collectors' interest. Recently, on the one hand, the increasing number of new releases has become hard to keep up with and, on the other, the prices of many obsolete diecast models have risen beyond the average collector's budget. As a result, a number of people have been turning to classic plastic, which has an appeal all of its own.

This book will prove invaluable to those collectors who are considering a move into plastic toys and models, and is likely to provide food for thought for many others...

Mike Forbes
Editor of *Diecast Collector* magazine

ACKNOWLEDGEMENTS

Some of the material contained in this book originally appeared in magazine articles and is reproduced by kind permission of Mike Forbes, editor of *Diecast Collector* and Lindsey Amrani, editor of *Model Collector*.

The author would like to express his thanks to the following collectors who kindly allowed photographs of their models to be used:

Alex J. Cameron
Douglas R. Kelly
Keith Schneider
Bruce Sterling

'Life in plastic is fantastic!' proclaimed the 1997 chart hit, 'Barbie Girl'. That was a sentiment the toy industry would have readily endorsed in the 1950s, as the advantages of plastic were becoming apparent – strength, ease of moulding into complex shapes and, most of all, low cost and ready availability compared to other raw materials. Initially, dolls were the most obvious toys to benefit from the use of plastic, but soon plastic moulding was widespread throughout the industry, not least in the manufacture of toy cars.

However, while the history of Dinky Toys, Corgi Toys and other makes of diecast metal cars has been covered in exhaustive detail in many books and magazine articles, comparatively little has been written about plastic toy cars. This book aims to provide some background information about the companies that made these toys, and to introduce the reader to the huge variety of vehicles that were modelled during the 1950s and early 1960s in Europe, America and elsewhere in the world.

Plastics in the toy industry

Plastics have been around since as far back as 1870 when celluloid was patented, but it was really only after the Second World War that they emerged as an economical and practical raw material. The reason was that the lack of natural rubber during the war stimulated scientists to develop synthetic substitutes. With the change over from a war-time to a peace-time economy, considerable quantities of these were readily available and many new applications were found, not least within the toy industry. A further stimulus to the use of plastics was the banning of metal for toy production during the Korean War of 1951.

In any case, by the mid-1950s traditional tin toys had had their day: they were beginning to look old-fashioned, while the number of sharp edges on them gave rise to safety concerns. Even in Germany, which had led the world in tin toy manufacture since the nineteenth century, tastes were changing. In the early 1960s, the association of German toy retailers advised its members not to sell tin toys for safety reasons and to stock plastic ones instead.

At first, plastic toys were mainly items such as rattles, balls, building blocks, dolls and dolls' furniture. Plastic was obviously ideally suited to these: it could be moulded in bright colours without the need for painting and was virtually unbreakable. As injection-moulding techniques improved, it was not long before more realistic plastic toys appeared. Being lighter than diecast metal and easier to mould into curved shapes than tinplate, cellulose acetate proved ideal for model cars powered by battery or clockwork motors. However, the disadvantage of this material was that the toy tended to 'warp' and become misshapen, and cellulose acetate was gradually superseded by polystyrene, with polythene being used for 'soft plastic' toys.

The sheer variety of toys available which were made of plastics led to a ready acceptance of these materials by a buying public starved of new toys during the Second World War and the years of austerity that followed. In 1961, the trade journal, *British Plastics,* estimated that in the decade between 1950 and 1960 sales of plastic toys had increased from under £2 million to approximately £8.5 million. In the same period, sales of metal toys grew at a slower rate, from nearly £11 million to £14 million. On the basis of these figures, the journal concluded that "plastics have established themselves … to such an extent that it is difficult to imagine what things were like before their advent."

Plastic in the collectors' market

When the hobby of collecting obsolete toys really took off in a big way in the 1980s, plastic toys were overlooked as the value of diecast models by Dinky, Corgi and Matchbox rose inexorably. There were, perhaps, two exceptions to this trend. Firstly, certain plastic construction kits by the likes of Airfix and Revell commanded considerable prices from specialist collectors so long as they were unmade and in their original packaging – which to some eyes defeats the purpose of an assembly kit! Secondly, in the USA, the 1/24 scale model cars sold, or given away, via car dealerships as promotional items have long been highly prized by collectors.

In the last few years, though, toy collectors have taken a much wider interest in the once neglected area of plastic toy cars. It's not hard to see why. Prices for obsolete diecast cars and for Japanese tin toys have put many of these items beyond the reach of the average enthusiast's budget. Toys such as these, particularly in mint condition with original boxes, now tend to sell via specialist auction houses

This
1/32 scale
Simca Aronde P60
is one of the most sought-after
models from the French Minialuxe company.
A mint and boxed example fetched a price of £280 on eBay
in February 2007.

always been a few careful children who preferred to keep their Dinky or Corgi toys in their original boxes instead of running them across the school playground, few would think of holding onto a 'cheap' plastic toy. The fact that plastic toys are more easily broken than their metal counterparts also makes survival less likely. Of course, it is precisely the challenge of seeking out something hard to find that is part of the appeal of the collecting hobby.

Plastic model cars have been manufactured in practically every European country. Many small companies in Britain branched into plastic after the Second World War, and some major ones, too, like Tri-ang and Wells-Brimtoy. Mainland Europe was also quick to see how plastics were ideally suited to model cars – particularly France, with Norev, Minialuxe and many other smaller ranges; Germany, with its large Gama models and smaller scale Wiking and Siku series; Spain, with Paya and Roco; Italy, with Ingap and Politoys, and so on. Even smaller countries like Austria, Denmark and Czechoslovakia have been active in this field. One place more than anywhere else became famous for plastic toy production: Hong Kong, whose products tended to be disseminated throughout the world under the brand names of toy importing and distribution companies rather than under the names of the makers themselves.

One of the challenges to collectors who are interested in plastic cars is that information can be hard to come by as relatively little has been published on the subject. While this volume is an attempt to rectify the situation, it makes no claim to be a complete history of plastic toy cars. Even to suggest that such a book could ever be written would be over-optimistic, and with such a vast field to choose from, it has been necessary to be selective. The general approach taken has been to focus on toys and models which are based on real, identifiable prototype vehicles, rather than those which are generic playthings.

rather than at collectors' fairs. This has led enthusiasts to seek out the hitherto undervalued items made of plastic. Today collectors are realising that these toys often have as much charm and realism as those fashioned from more traditional raw materials, and prices are rising accordingly.

In fact, because plastic toys were underrated for so long, it is likely that many of them are actually scarcer than comparable diecast or tin toys, simply because their survival rate is lower. While there have

The British Tri-ang company was one of the first to launch a range of plastic cars after the Second World War. The 'No.2 Saloon' resembles an American Buick; five different variations are shown on this catalogue page.

In terms of size, many plastic cars were made in small scales (i.e. between 1/72-1/86 to go with OO/HO Scale model railways); many were the standard 1/43 size used for diecast cars (though in practice this could be anywhere between 1/40 and 1/50); the larger friction drive or battery-operated ones varied from 1/32 to 1/20 scale. However, as these cars were meant as toys rather than accurate models, scales could be very approximate. The captions to many of the photographs in this book accordingly give the length of the vehicle rather than its scale.

The histories of a few plastic toy companies have already been covered in other books, such as Norev of France, Wiking and Siku of Germany, early American plastics, Lego and other Danish brands. These areas are therefore not covered in depth here, allowing more space to be devoted to other toy companies about which little or nothing has appeared in print. Most of the items pictured have their original boxes, as without these it can sometimes be difficult to identify the manufacturer, particularly in the case of some of the more obscure pieces.

How much is it worth?

It is impossible to give an accurate valuation for many vintage toys, as in many cases an item is worth whatever a collector is willing to pay for it. Nevertheless, the approximate prices indicated will serve as a guide to the relative rarity of each model shown. As with all collectable toys, prices are for items in mint condition with original, undamaged boxes. Unboxed items are likely to fetch no more than half the price of boxed ones. Unless otherwise indicated, it can be assumed that models pictured without boxes would have been sold loose.

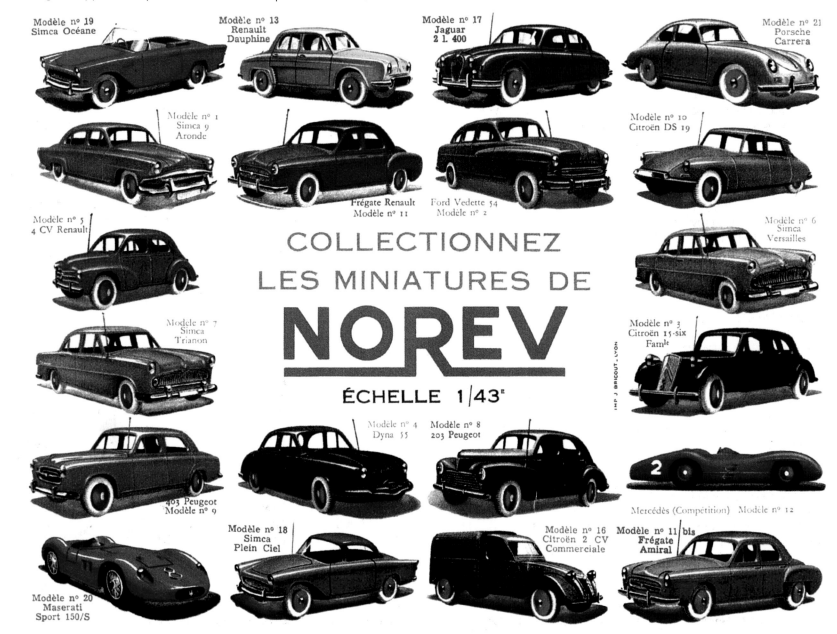

Modèle n° 19
Simca Océane

Modèle n° 13
Renault
Dauphine

Modèle n° 17
Jaguar
2 l. 400

Modèle n° 21
Porsche
Carrera

Modèle n° 1
Simca 9
Aronde

Modèle n° 10
Citroën DS 19

Frégate Renault
Modèle n° 11

Ford Vedette 54
Modèle n° 2

Modèle n° 5
4 CV Renault

Modèle n° 6
Simca
Versailles

COLLECTIONNEZ
LES MINIATURES DE
NOREV
ÉCHELLE 1/43ᵉ

Modèle n° 7
Simca
Trianon

Modèle n° 3
Citroën 15-six
Famle

Modèle n° 4
Dyna 55

Modèle n° 8
203 Peugeot

403 Peugeot
Modèle n° 9

Mercédès (Compétition)   Modèle n° 12

Modèle n° 20
Maserati
Sport 150/S

Modèle n° 18
Simca
Plein Ciel

Modèle n° 16
Citroën 2 CV
Commerciale

Modèle n° 11 bis
Frégate
Amiral

IMP J BRICOUT, LYON

GREAT BRITAIN

As early as December 1947, the trade journal 'British Plastics' described the plastics industry as 'overwhelmed by the widespread acceptance of plastics by the toy industry.' This was partly because of the continuing shortages of metal for toy production and partly because of the huge pent-up demand for new toys after the Second World War, which meant that almost anything would sell.

As a result, numerous manufacturers quickly became involved in the production of plastic toys, including cars. Some were already in the plastics business and started applying their expertise to toys as a means of expanding their product line; others had many years of experience of making toys from traditional materials like tinplate, and changed to plastics as a way of economising on production costs or overcoming metal shortages.

Palitoy

Among the earliest post-war toy vehicles were a group of four, advertised to the toy trade in 1948 by Cascelloid of Leicester, who made dolls under the trademark Palitoy. The company was formed in 1911 by Mr. A. E. Pallett. Palitoy's bus, van, saloon car and coupé were available either with free-rolling wheels or with a clockwork motor inside. The van and bus are simple, generic designs, but the saloon is recognisably a Jaguar – possibly copied from a contemporary Crescent diecast – while the coupé is an American Ford. What they lack in realism, they more than make up for in charm, particularly when found with their original boxes, which are designed to look like a garage lock-up. The delivery van can be found with various paper stickers, while a variation has been seen with a single battery-operated headlight sticking out of the radiator. Pressure on the bonnet causes contact to be made and the bulb lights up. Another Cascelloid toy, based on the same principle, was a toy dog whose nose lit up when its tail was pushed in!

Three other Palitoy cars, dating from 1950–51, are of interest to collectors, as they are based on real prototypes which the diecast manufacturers of the time largely overlooked. The Triumph Mayflower and the Sunbeam Talbot were both clockwork-powered, whereas the larger Austin A70 Hampshire had a battery-driven motor. This was marketed by the Ever Ready company, for it was obviously a good move for a battery maker to encourage sales of battery toys!

Beeju

Another company that quickly saw the potential of plastic in toy car production was EVB Plastics of Salfords, Surrey. Using the tradename 'Beeju', EVB advertised a simple plastic fire engine as early as 1948, to be followed by an extensive series of lorries, retailing at only 1/- (5p) each. Most of these had a common chassis but the series also included a Daimler ambulance.

Also dating from this period is a delightful set of four simple racing cars, packed in a yellow box marked 'Service Garage' which could open out into a petrol station. Beeju had aspirations beyond the UK market, too. In 1949, a 4.5 inch clockwork-powered American car was advertised to the toy trade, available in coupé, saloon and cabriolet versions. The text of the advertisement is in French, Spanish and English, suggesting that Beeju had these export markets in mind.

Victory

Many of these plastic toys are attractive novelties, but only a few could claim to be scale models. The 1/20 scale electrically-powered cars produced by Victory Industries are in a different league. This is one of the few plastic toy companies whose history has been researched extensively, and enthusiast Malcolm Parker has published his findings on a website. Victory had discovered another big advantage of plastic: as it was light it could be used for larger-scale battery-powered cars, as there was less strain on the motor. With larger scales came greater realism, amply demonstrated by Victory's model of the 1949 Morris Minor.

The Minor was followed by other British cars of the period – Vauxhall Velox, Austin A40, MGTF, Hillman Minx, Standard Ten, Triumph TR2/3, MGA and so on. From 1957 onwards, though, the company concentrated on its VIP Electric Model Roadway system. What was particularly noteworthy about the Victory cars was that they were made by arrangement with the real manufacturers and used in showrooms as promotional models – perhaps the first British example of a practice that was widespread in the USA.

TOURER
Topédo decouvert
Turismo

COUPE
Coupé
Coupe

SALOON
Conduite intérieure
Coche Salon

'BEEJU'

PLASTIC CLOCKWORK TOYS

BEAUTIFUL TWO-COLOUR PLASTIC
MECHANISED CARS. Size 4½" x 1¾". Passengers to Tourer. Drivers to Coupé and Saloon.

E.V.B. PLASTICS LTD

PEAR TREE HILL, BRIGHTON ROAD
SALFORDS, REDHILL
SURREY, ENG.

Telephone: Horley 1067
Telegrams: Eveebee, Redhill

These brightly-coloured clockwork plastic cars were announced to the toy trade in 1949. The makers EVB Plastics Ltd., used the trademark 'Beeju'.

Mettoy

The USA influenced the British plastic toy industry in other ways, too. One of the big American companies, the Ideal Toy Corporation, made an arrangement with O and M Kleeman Limited which allowed some of Ideal's plastic toys to be sold in the UK. These were often quite elaborate, coming with numerous accessories to enhance play value. The Decorator's Truck, for example, carried a load of small paint pots, a paint brush and a miniature ladder. In 1948, Henry Ullman, son of the founder of the Mettoy company which had been making tin toys since the 1930s, visited the US and returned with the idea of producing toys in plastic. Mettoy had made some Dinky Toy-sized cars such as a Standard Vanguard, the mould of which was converted for use with plastic, and a new series of plastic trucks with an Austin cab was launched. Larger-sized models followed, some with friction mechanisms and other more elaborate ones with electric motors or lighting, the Jaguar 2.4 being the summit of Mettoy's achievement in this field. This featured a robust moulded bodyshell with fittings such as the radiator grille and bumpers being added in diecast metal. The distinctive Jaguar bonnet mascot wasn't forgotten either.

Timpo

While not as big a player in the post-war toy market as Mettoy, Timpo also deserves a mention here. The name simply stands for Toy Importers Limited, founded in 1938 by Mr Sally Gawrylowicz. Very soon afterwards, war conditions made toy importation impossible and Timpo started making its own toys – managing to continue during the war by developing a composition material as a substitute for metal. After the war, Timpo was quick to introduce diecast metal cars and trucks, though they were very crudely made. Timpo next turned to plastic, making some friction-driven trucks under the Elmont name. While these were little more than a minor footnote in model car history, Timpo nevertheless went on to develop its plastic moulding skills and successfully continued making soldiers and cowboy figures until 1979.

Wells-Brimtoy

Like Mettoy, Wells-Brimtoy had a long track record of producing tinplate toy cars. The company was formed in 1932, when British Metal and Toy Manufacturers (founded in 1914) was taken over by A. Wells and Co. (founded in 1919). Wells-Brimtoy launched its 'Pocketoy' series in 1952, combining the latest plastic moulding methods with traditional lithographed tinplate. Most of this series consisted of simple Bedford trucks with very colourful bodies but there were a few plastic cars dating from 1951, notably the Morris Minor. The Brimtoy is of interest to collectors as it, along with the much more expensive version by Victory, is one of very few replicas of the early split-screen Minor.

Brimtoy obviously maintained a close connection with the Vauxhall-Bedford company, as most of its trucks were based on Bedfords. In addition to the small (3.5 inch) Pocketoys, other larger Bedfords were made, still incorporating a good deal of tinplate, often with lethally sharp edges which would probably have them banned as children's toys today for safety reasons!

If Mettoy's Jaguar was its pièce de résistance, Brimtoy's equivalent was the Vauxhall Cresta, with its very realistic moulded body and remote-control battery box. This was featured as a Christmas gift suggestion in *Vauxhall Motorist*, Vauxhall's in-house magazine, in December 1957.

Tri-ang Minic

However, one British toy company made more plastic toy cars than all the others put together: Tri-ang, which, along with Meccano Limited, dominated the UK toy market for decades. The company's origins go back to the 1870s when the Lines family began producing wooden toys and rocking horses. After the First World War, three of Joseph Lines' sons decided to set up on their own, coming up with the Tri-ang name as three lines form a triangle. After the Second World War, Tri-ang developed into a toy empire, with several factories in England and Wales, soon followed by factories as far afield as Canada, Australia, New Zealand and South Africa.

Tri-ang was quick to see the potential of plastic for toy production, especially for model aircraft. As early as 1947, the Penguin series of plastic cars appeared, powered – fittingly for these austere times – not by an electric or clockwork motor but by a simple elastic band. The first was a Maserati racing car, which drew

Tri-ang Minic Major models were fitted with 'Push and Go' friction mechanisms.

M.210	Mercedes Racer. 6¼" (15·6 cms)	**M.222**	Fire Engine. 6¼" (15·6 cms)	
M.215	Delivery Van. 5½" (14 cms)	**M.224**	B.O.A.C. Coach. 8¼" (20·6 cms)	
M.216	Ambulance. 5½" (14 cms)	**M.225**	Steam Roller. (New Type) 5¾" (13·8 cms)	
M.217	Petrol Tanker. 5½" (14 cms)	**M.227**	Cooper Racing Car. 6" (15·2 cms)	
M.218	Taxi. 5½" (14 cms)	**M.228**	New Double Decker Bus. 7¼" (18·4 cms)	
M.221	Black Maria. 5½" (13 cms)	**M.229**	G.P.O. Mail Van. 5½" (13 cms)	

M225 is clockwork, remainder have powerful 'Push & Go' units.

considerable attention in the pages of *British Plastics* in November 1947. "The whole body is moulded in cellulose acetate in one piece and is designed to accommodate the metal chassis on which is mounted the operating mechanism. Up to six bodies are moulded per shot, and strong but light models can be manufactured in a variety of colours. The first of this series is the Penguin racing car, based on the Maserati racer. The popularity of this model is shown by the fact that over a million of them have already been sold." Others followed, sought after today as they are based on unusual subjects: an American Ford, an Armstrong Siddeley Hurricane and a Jowett Javelin.

Beside these, Tri-ang's traditional toy car line – the tinplate Minic series – looked old-fashioned. Gradually, the old Minics were superseded by new models with plastic bodies – though to avoid any negative reactions from buyers the word 'plastic' was never used in catalogues, which referred to 'moulded bodies' instead. Designated 'Minic Series II', these were more sophisticated than the rather basic Penguins. The mainstay of the range was a car described simply as the 'No.2 saloon', though it was probably based on a 1949 Buick, designed to appeal to the American export market.

While Tri-ang was pioneering plastic in toy car production, a much smaller company, Rovex, was founded by Alexander Gregory Vanetzian in 1946. Rovex secured a contract to supply plastic toys to Marks and Spencer and these included a few small cars about three inches in length, yet powered by a compact clockwork motor. Marks and Spencer also commissioned a plastic battery-driven train set. Seeing the potential of this product, Lines Brothers took over the firm in 1951 and developed Tri-ang Railways which soon gave serious competition to Meccano Limited's long-established Hornby Dublo series. In 1954, Rovex moved to a new factory in Margate.

Having expanded its plastic manufacturing facilities, Tri-ang next launched a cheaper series of toys, the Minic 'Push and Go' series. The best of these were friction-powered cars around four inches in length, based on popular cars of the period like the Morris Oxford, Austin A40 Devon, Hillman Minx and Standard Vanguard. Many others were commercial vehicles with a simple non-prototypical cab design and fitted with many different loads – timber, coal, cement, container lorry and so on. The range grew quickly in so many different scales that Tri-ang made an attempt to rationalise it in its 1961 catalogue by dividing it into the Major, Minor and Minimus series. The Major models were between 5½ and 7½ inches long and, perhaps because of their larger size, were often moulded in two halves, leaving a join down the middle. The small Minimus models were a little bigger than the Lesney Matchbox series, and the bodyshells often had solid windows to conceal the friction motor inside. Most 'Push and Go' toys are not very realistic, but some are sought after as they are based on interesting subjects: No M219 in the Major series, for instance, is a model of a Ford 100E Escort estate car, while the smaller range included a Bentley Continental Coupé, a Morris Minibus and a Standard Vanguard Vignale Estate Car, none of which was available in diecast form.

Meanwhile, at the top end of the toy car market, Tri-ang offered a series of 1/20 scale electric cars, which took further the earlier Victory concept. Tri-ang's move into this field effectively killed off any remaining demand for the Victory series and led that company to focus instead

in the *NEW* super gloss plastic

MINIC LIMITED, CANTERBURY, KENT

The Minic 1/20 scale cars were among the most accurate plastic models. They were electrically-powered.

on developing the 'VIP' electric roadway system. The Tri-ang range included many desirable vehicles like the Austin Healey 100, MGA, Triumph Herald Coupé and the Bentley Continental convertible.

The standard of the Minic 1/20 series was never surpassed as several factors led British toy companies to develop in other directions. The main one was that Hong Kong companies were able to produce battery-operated toy cars far more cheaply, and as a result, UK toy manufacturers began to take more interest in developing slot car racing systems which were much more fun to play with – not only the hugely successful Scalextric range but others like Minic Motorways, Airfix and Champion.

The last significant plastic range made by Tri-ang was the Minix series of 1/76 scale cars, launched in 1965. Designed to accompany Tri-ang railways, the Minix range included many of the cars familiar on British roads in the late 1960s: Ford Anglia and Corsair, Morris 1100, Vauxhall Viva and Victor, Triumph 2000, Austin A60 and 1800, Sunbeam

This plastic bus first appeared in 1958 and was still on sale 45 years later!

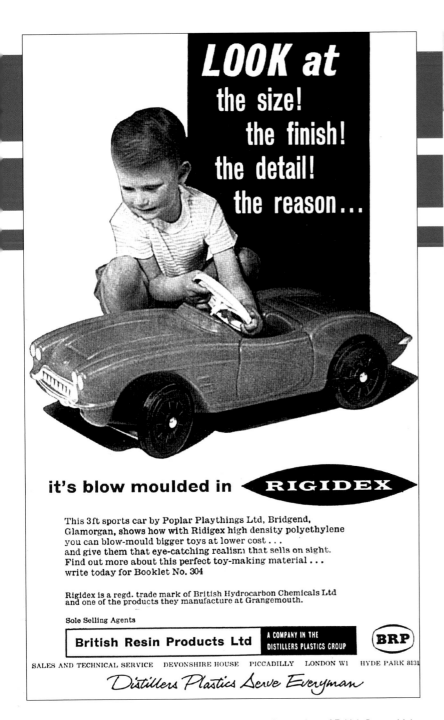

LOOK at
the size!
the finish!
the detail!
the reason...

it's blow moulded in RIGIDEX

This 3ft sports car by Poplar Playthings Ltd, Bridgend,
Glamorgan, shows how with Ridigex high density polyethylene
you can blow-mould bigger toys at lower cost . . .
and give them that eye-catching realism that sells on sight.
Find out more about this perfect toy-making material . . .
write today for Booklet No. 304

Rigidex is a regd. trade mark of British Hydrocarbon Chemicals Ltd
and one of the products they manufacture at Grangemouth.

Sole Selling Agents

British Resin Products Ltd | A COMPANY IN THE DISTILLERS PLASTICS GROUP | BRP

SALES AND TECHNICAL SERVICE   DEVONSHIRE HOUSE   PICCADILLY   LONDON W1   HYDE PARK 8131

Distillers Plastics Serve Everyman

Poplar Playthings of Bridgend, Glamorgan, was one of a number of British firms which specialised in 'soft' plastic toys for younger children. The car shown is a Chevrolet Corvette.

Alpine, Hillman Minx and Imp, Simca 1300 and the Ford Thames Van. According to Tri-ang expert Pat Hammond, some 10 million examples of Minix cars were churned out before production ceased in 1972.

Polythene toys

During the 1960s, the bulk of plastic toy production in Britain lay in another sector of the market altogether: playthings aimed at three to ten year-olds. By 1961, British plastic toy production had increased four-fold since 1950 and was currently worth £9 million, mainly consisting of toys made from 'softer' plastics – polythene and polypropylene. One trade journal identified a 'clear trend towards working models of earth-moving equipment and other types of machinery used by road and building contractors, such as bulldozers, cranes and the like.' Some of the many firms active in this field were Rosedale Associated Manufacturers, based in Glamorgan and well-known for its dolls; Raphael Lipkin of South Lambeth Road SW8 (Pippin Toys); Cassidy Brothers (Casdon) of Blackpool; Cherilea of Kirkham, Lancashire and Poplar Playthings of Bridgend, Glamorgan. The latter advertised prominently in toy trade journals and among its many plastic vehicles were: a London bus (1958), a Mercedes Gullwing Police Car and Fire Chief's Car (1959), an MGA sports car, a Fire Engine copied from a Dinky Toy (1962) and a Ford Thames Trader (1963). Amazingly, the moulds for some of these survived: toy outlets in the early 2000s were still selling the bus under the name 'Springwell Mouldings'.

The fact that there is still a place for these simple plastic toys forty-five years after they first appeared speaks volumes for their appeal, even if the advertising slogan on the bus – 'Buy British Toys' – is something of an anachronism in an era where practically every plaything is manufactured in the Far East.

GREAT BRITAIN

Unknown Bluebird Record Car
Although it carries no identification marks, this could be an early Palitoy product, based on Malcolm Campbell's 1935 Bluebird VI record car which was modelled in metal by Britains.
Price guide: £30

Palitoy Ford Coupé ▶
Part of a series first announced in 1948, this coupé is loosely based on an American Ford. It has a key on one side to wind up the clockwork motor. Scale is approximately 1/40th.
Price guide: £20

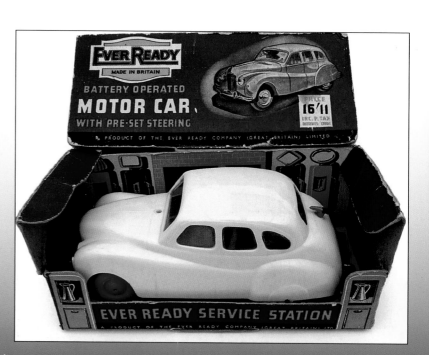

▲
Palitoy Jaguar
This simple Jaguar may have been copied from an early post-war diecast made by Die Casting Machine Tools (DCMT) and marketed by Crescent Toys.
Price guide: £20

Ever Ready Austin A70 Hampshire ▶
This model dates from 1950 and was made by Palitoy but distributed by Ever Ready batteries. Two versions have been seen, one of which has a hand control box which operates the car via a cable inserted through a hole in the bonnet. On the other, (pictured) the motor is ingeniously controlled by turning the boot handle. The Austin is also available in red or blue. Length: 7 inches.
Price guide: £60

Unknown Breakdown Truck ▶

The wheels fitted to this truck are similar to those on the Palitoys, suggesting it comes from the same stable. Clearly the maker was not bothered about keeping to a constant scale, as the car is much smaller than the truck!
Price guide: £15

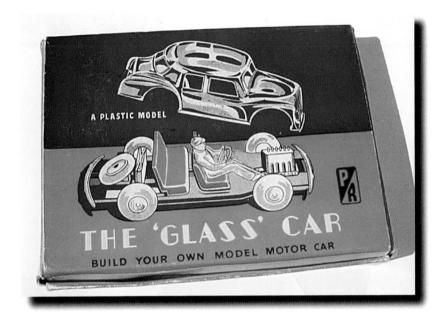

A PLASTIC MODEL

PR

THE 'GLASS' CAR

BUILD YOUR OWN MODEL MOTOR CAR

◀ **Glass Car**
▼ *This clip-together car is 4.25 inches long and is a generic design rather than a representation of any particular vehicle. Both the concept and the box style are based on the German Wiking 1/40 Volkswagen models, but this item is British-made.*
Price guide: £35

Kleeware PAINTERS & DECORATORS

Kleeware PAINTER'S & DECORATOR'S LORRY

A Kleeware PRODUCT

Complete with 14 PIECE HOME DECORATORS OUTFIT

◀ **Kleeware Painter's Truck**
This toy was originally sold in the USA by the Ideal Toy Corporation which, presumably, licensed Kleeware to market it in the UK. It came with paint pots and brushes. Length: 11.5 inches.
Price guide: £40

Beeju Bus

Beeju's series of small commercial vehicles included both single and double-decker buses. One appealing feature was the provision of a driver and passengers.
Price guide: £10

▼

▲

Beeju Racing Car set

This late 1940s set, made by EVB Plastics of Salfords, Surrey, consists of the same racing car in four different colours – red, light blue, green and yellow – contained in a box which folds out into a starting grid. The set is on show in the Hamilton Toy Museum, Callander, Scotland.
Price guide: £40

◄ ### Welsotoys Vauxhall Cresta

Vauxhall's luxury model, the Cresta, was introduced in 1955, the same year that Brimtoy started using a new trademark, 'Welsotoys'. The body of this eight inch-long model is entirely in plastic with grille, bonnet fittings and interior in tin. The car is powered by a battery-operated remote-control. Listed in 1957 at a price of £1.15 shillings (£1.75), the Cresta would have been an expensive toy for its day.
Price guide: £50

Fire Engine and Beeju Ambulance ►

The front of the ambulance is inspired by the early 1950s Daimler. The figures inside are borrowed from the fire engine, but they are so small that they can barely see through the windscreen!
Price guide: £10 each

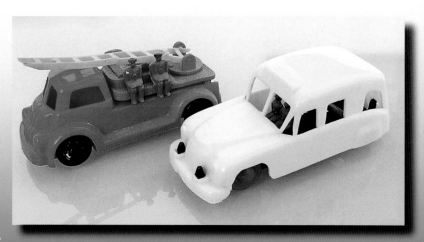

Brimtoy Zig-Zag car
As its name suggests, this six inch clockwork-powered car moves forward with a 'zig-zag' motion. The shape is loosely based on the pre-war Lincoln Zephyr, a car that would not have been a common sight on British roads. It comes in different colours and with various other box styles.
Price guide: £40

Brimtoy Pocketoy Bedford Transport Lorry ▶
Dating from 1951, this model illustrates the characteristic Brimtoy marriage of old and new materials, with plastic being used for the cab unit and lithographed tin for the box trailer. The cab design is based on a Bedford cab, also modelled by Dinky Toys.
Price guide: £70

Brimtoy Pocketoy Esso Tanker
Brimtoy also made some smaller, 3.5 inch trucks. The cab appears to be of a generic design. Quite common in unboxed condition, these Pocketoys are much harder to find with their original boxes.
Price guide: £25

Brimtoy Pocketoy Snack Bar

From 1954 onwards, Brimtoy issued the smaller trucks with this Bedford 'S' type cab style. Many different variations can be found, often with an opening feature, such as the fold-down counter on this snack bar. There was even a horse box with a horse's head that poked out at the back when a lever was turned!
Price guide: £30

Brimtoy Morris Minor

This 3.5 inch Minor first appeared in 1951, consisting simply of a plastic body clipped onto a tin base. It is one of the few replicas of the early 'split-screen' Morris Minor.
Price guide: £20

Wells Brimtoy Ford Prefect and Squire

These two plastic 2.5 inch-long Fords were supplied as part of a petrol station set. The V-shaped bonnet mascot indicates they are based on the post-1957 Ford 100E in saloon and estate car form.
Price guide: £5-£10 each (loose); £75 for boxed garage set

Unknown Cattle Truck

The cab unit is moulded in plastic while the trailer is in classic pre-war style with brightly-coloured lithographed decorations – in this case depicting pigs! The same maker also offered an Esso tanker and possibly other items too. Length: 6 inches.
Price guide: £25

Mettoy Austin Breakdown ▶

Four variations on this Austin were announced in Mettoy's 1953 catalogue: open truck, tipper, fire engine and breakdown. Length: 4.25 inches.
Price guide: £10

Mettoy Luxury Coach ◀

A larger (11 inch) and more elaborate model, with electric lighting, plastic figures and a rotating destination board. The transparent top can be removed to allow the driver and passenger figures to be repositioned as desired.
Price guide: £60

Mettoy Ambulance ▶

The cab is similar to the breakdown but the ambulance is in a larger scale (7 inches long). The same model also comes as a dark blue police van and the box illustrates both versions. The rear doors open.
Price guide: £50

Mettoy Fire Engine ◀

Similar in scale to the ambulance, the fire engine has a bell which rings as the toy is pushed along. The cab is loosely based on a Bedford. Length: 7 inches.
Price guide: £40

Mettoy Jaguar 2.4 ▶

This is the most sophisticated of the numerous plastic cars made by Mettoy. It is 9.5 inches long and has a plastic body with diecast metal used for the base, bumpers and trim details – including the bonnet mascot. The batteries are inserted in a compartment underneath, covered by a plastic lid which is often missing on unboxed examples.
Price guide: £75

▲ Marx Motorway Cars

These 5 inch American-style estate cars have a powerful clockwork motor and were supplied in a set with track which they could run on.
Price guide: £10 each

Marx Ford Zephyr Police Car ▶

This Zephyr looks as if it was copied from the Corgi Toy diecast. It was made in the Marx factory in Swansea, Wales – which was in fact situated on the same industrial estate as the Corgi factory!
Price guide: £50
(Courtesy Alex J. Cameron)

Marx Pontiac
Another product of the British Marx factory, this 9.5 inch American car represents a 1950 Pontiac. Like the Zephyr, it is controlled from a hand-held battery box.
Price guide: £45

Victory Morris Minors
Two versions of the 1/20 scale electrically-powered Morris Minor by Victory, the red car with the 'split screen' being the earlier one. Tri-ang later made a similar range of 1/20 scale battery-operated cars, of which the Austin Taxi is an example.
Price guide: £100 each
(Courtesy Bruce Sterling).

Penguin Series Armstrong Siddeley Hurricane
Appearing in 1947, the Penguin series was one of the earliest ranges of plastic toy cars. Unusually, these cars were powered by an elastic band which was wound up by the starting handle at the front.
Price guide: £40

Minic Morris Eight
This pre-war design was reintroduced in 1946 and kept buyers satisfied until the arrival of the new Minor in 1948. This Minic model has a clockwork motor.
Price guide: £40

Minic Austin A40 van
From 1954 onwards, Tri-ang developed a large series of 'Push and Go' cars, the most interesting ones being based on contemporary cars like the Standard Vanguard, Morris Oxford and Hillman Minx. The colourful 'Evening News' van is one of the most sought-after.
Price guide: £50

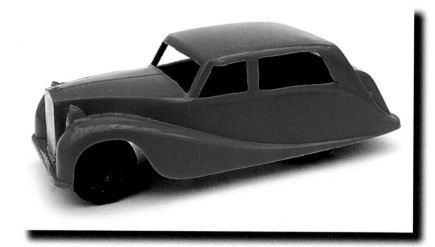

Minic Rolls Royce
Yet another Minic series consisted of smaller, c.2.75 inch cars, such as this Rolls Royce. The friction motors did not work very efficiently.
Price guide: £8

Minic Jaguar Mk VII
One advantage of the Minic 'Push and Go' range was that it included numerous cars that were not modelled in diecast form, such as this Jaguar.
Price guide: £10

Minic MGA
Unlike the simple 'Push and Go' cars, the 1/20 scale series of the late 1950s consisted of highly realistic replicas. Ingeniously, the gear lever in this MGA acts as the on-off switch for the electric motor. The batteries are inserted underneath the car.
Price guide: £100+

Tudor Rose Estate Car ▶

There could hardly be a simpler toy than this 4 inch station wagon, loosely based on the American 'woody' type.
Price guide: £5

▲

Tudor Rose American Car

Like the station wagon, this Tudor Rose car is in the American style, but to a larger scale (7 inches).
Price guide: £10

▲

Tudor Rose Ferrari

This 7.25 inch sports car has been variously identified as an Austin Healey and a Ferrari Barchetta, loosely resembling both in certain respects.
Price guide: £20

◀ **Tudor Rose Euclid Tipper**

Described on the box as 'almost indestructible', this clockwork Euclid 15 Ton Rear Dump Truck takes its inspiration from a popular Dinky Toy of the period.
Length: 7.5 inches.
Price guide: £15

GREAT BRITAIN

Mechanical Horse ▶

The colours used on this 'flexible polythene' toy reflect the age group it was aimed at, but it remains a pretty accurate likeness nonetheless. The box carries the inscription 'Richdon Toys – International Products, London N21'. Length: 12 inches.
Price guide: £20

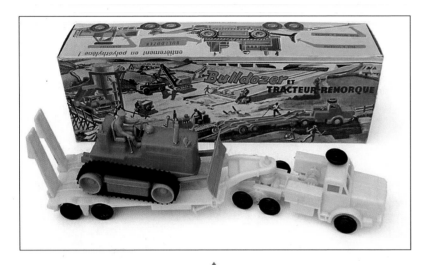

Mighty Antar and Bulldozer ▲

This 16 inch-long Mighty Antar has similarities to the Dinky Supertoy model. It has an operating winch and many small components – there's even an opening compartment containing a selection of tiny plastic tools. Though marked 'Made in England', the box copy is in French, suggesting the toy was exported.
Price guide: £30

Citroën DS and Jaguar MkII ▲

The Citroën seems to be based on a Corgi Toy and the Jaguar on a Dinky. Both are the same size as their diecast equivalents and are marked simply 'Made in England'.
Price guide: £15 each

FRANCE

Situated in the département of l'Ain in the east of France, the town of Oyonnax is the centre of the French plastics industry. In the eighteenth century, the town prospered through manufacturing combs from wood and horn. The introduction of celluloid in 1880 marked the start of an industry which grew to be of such significance after the Second World War that the area round Oyonnax is today known as plastics vallée, with some 1500 companies involved in the design and manufacture of plastic products.

1953 was a landmark year in the development of the French plastics industry, as the first trade fair (Foire des Plastiques) took place in Oyonnax, attracting 10,000 buyers, wholesalers and importers from all over Europe. On the first day alone, orders were placed for nine million items.

Norev

Among the exhibitors at the fair were many large and small toy companies from this part of France, but all of them could be said, to a greater or lesser extent, to take their lead from Norev, based in the nearby city of Lyon. Joseph Veron had worked in the plastics industry for Rhône-Poulenc, a leading chemical and pharmaceutical group founded in 1928 and still very much in business, now being known as Rhodia. The company had developed a plastic composition trademarked 'Rhodialite' and Monsieur Veron saw the potential of this in the production of cheap toys, which would be ideally suited to the austere climate of the post-war market.

By reversing the letters of his surname, Veron created the 'Norev' brand and ventured into toy production with novelties such as toy watches, a miniature sewing machine and a doll's feeding set. The first cars were a colourful set of four vehicles in about 1/87 scale – saloon, convertible, van and open truck, supplied in a tin garage lithographed in red and yellow. It was in 1953 that Norev really found its niche, as it was in that year that a range of 1/43 scale cars was launched, starting with a Simca Aronde. As they were made of plastic, the Norevs could beat Dinky on price and they were soon so popular that a new factory was built in the rue 4 Août in the industrial suburb of Villeurbanne, which Norev claimed was the most modern toy factory in Europe, employing over 400 people.

As well as being toys, Norevs were a fitting advertisement for the versatility of Rhône-Poulenc's raw materials, and a paper tag was attached to each car stating that 'Norev has moulded this coachwork

One of Norev's many clever marketing ideas was to supply toy shops with paper bags advertising the Norev range.

in Rhodialite'. Far from seeing plastic as a cheap substitute for diecast metal, Norev regarded the plastic construction of its toys as their main selling point, and catalogues are full of reminders such as 'Norev miniatures are not painted; the colour is in the material; therefore they always remain fresh.' One catalogue even boasts that the colours are 'guaranteed unalterable even if the car is scraped with a file or knife' – a challenge which some mischievous children no doubt took up!

The downside, however, was that a chemical reaction could take place when two plastic components were stuck together, causing discolouration. Moreover, like so many early plastic toys, Norevs tend to warp – though this problem actually affects some of the later, rather than the earlier, Norevs.

Among other selling points were that the cars were fitted with a radio aerial and most could be found in both free-running and friction-drive versions. The catalogue advised buyers to "own all the Norev miniatures in double: a mechanical one to play with and another so that you will always have a collection of fresh models which you will be proud of later." Any child with the foresight to follow this advice will have cause to be thankful today!

Like most French manufacturers, Norev initially drew its subjects almost exclusively from contemporary French cars which children would recognise. By 1956, the range included a Ford Vedette, Citroën Six Familiale, Dyna Panhard, Renault 4CV and Fregate, Simca Versailles and Trianon, Peugeot 203 and 403, Citroën DS and – the first non-French subject – a Mercedes racing car. From 1957 onwards, there was also a parallel Micro-Miniature series in 1/86 scale. The range grew rapidly: from 12 in 1956 to 96 by 1964, by which time Norev could now offer a replica of practically every well-known car by Citroën, Renault, Simca and Peugeot, with a good selection of German and Italian cars too. There was even a British Jaguar 2.4, later followed by three Fords – the Anglia, Classic and Cortina – plus the Mini, Austin and MG 1100s, and the Rolls Royce Silver Shadow.

By 1971, though, plastic cars were falling out of fashion and Norev launched its Jet-Car diecast series, though most of the same vehicles continued to be made in plastic for some time. The Norev output is so vast that it requires a book to itself, and French enthusiast Didier Beaujardin has duly obliged with a two volume history of the company (see bibliography) which methodically catalogues all issues right up to the present day – for Norev continues to have a significant presence on the model car market, though it now caters for adult collectors and, of course, sub-contracts manufacture to China.

Minialuxe

Norev had a close rival in Minialuxe, a range which, until recently, received less attention from collectors, partly because much less was known about it than Norev, whose history can be well-documented through annual catalogues and other publications such as *Norevenement*, a trade newsletter.

The makers of Minialuxe were Etablissements Grand Clément of 170 rue Anatole France, Oyonnax. Although one early trade catalogue claims that "our company, founded in 1903, was the first to try to solve the problem of making miniature cars from rhodialite", it seems that the first models did not appear until 1954, a year after Norev launched

its range. Inevitably, there was a certain amount of overlap: among the early issues were a Simca Aronde and a Renault Frégate, both of which were poorer replicas that the comparable Norevs.

Nevertheless, Minialuxe had plenty of ideas of its own and was certainly not just trying to copy what Norev did. For one thing, some of the less obvious French cars of the period were modelled, notably the Peugeot 203 in estate car (familiale) form and the Hotchkiss Grégoire. Unlike Norev, Minialuxe also produced numerous accessories to go with its cars, such as petrol pumps, a garage ramp, traffic policeman, traffic lights and so on. The most significant difference, however, was that Minialuxe produced a range of cars in 1/32 as well as 1/43 scale, a size which allowed for more detail. The first two were a Simca Versailles and a Citroën DS 19, followed by a Peugeot 403 in July 1956 and a Renault Dauphine in September. These featured friction motors, window glazing, plated grilles and bumpers and, in most cases, an opening boot. The Dauphine even had, like the real one, a drop-down compartment at the front containing a spare wheel. By the standards of the period, these were quite advanced features.

There were differences, too, in the marketing tools used by both companies. Norev was very good at publicity, supplying toy shops with paper bags that advertised Norevs and producing sales aids like an imposing metal ferris wheel with cradles to hold Norev models. Members of the Norev collectors' club received a small plastic badge. Minialuxe, for its part, supplied its models for use in promotions for various products like coffee (Cafés Brésilia), clothes (Vétements Bayard), chocolate (Delespaul) and the Tintin comic. Some of these promotional models had a brand name stamped in gold lettering on the roof or side of the model.

Unlike Norev, Minialuxe sometimes used other distributors to sell its products. Some models appeared in boxes marked 'Punch', who handled various toy car ranges. The cryptic 'MV' logo on early Minialuxe boxes which has long puzzled French collectors stands for Verpiot et Mameaux, a firm of toy distributors with offices in Lyon and Paris.

One advertising ploy used by both Norev and Minialuxe – and numerous other French toy companies – was the 'buvard', a sheet of blotting paper advertising a product. Dating from the days when children used fountain pens in school, these were popular giveaways at the time and are prized by collectors today.

In the course of the 1960s, the battle between Minialuxe and Norev intensified. Minialuxe made much of its innovation of spring suspension which it called 'Minia-stable' – hardly an appropriate term as the plastic strips which acted as springs were so flexible that the models lost their stability! More successful was the announcement in 1964 of a series of veteran cars, 'Les Tacots', which ran to 34 1/43 scale cars. Many manufacturers at this time followed the lead of the Matchbox Yesteryear series and modelled cars of the 1900s and earlier, but these are out of fashion with collectors at the moment.

In the late 1960s, many of the cars in the Norev range were duplicated by Minialuxe and it became clear that the market – which was already shrinking – could not sustain two similar ranges. Norev turned to diecast metal and Minialuxe was about to do the same, advertising a Berliet Stradair articulated tanker in 1971. This did reach

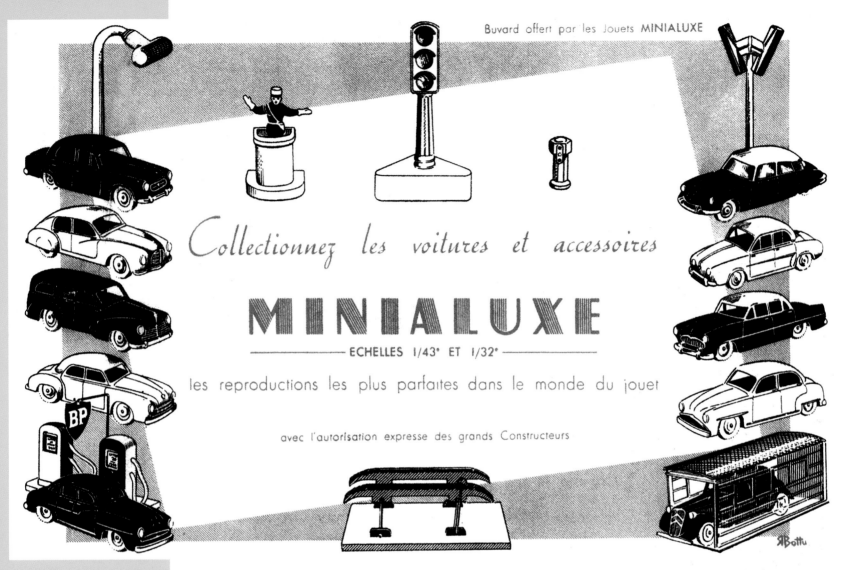

Buvard offert par les Jouets MINIALUXE

Collectionnez les voitures et accessoires

MINIALUXE

ECHELLES 1/43° ET 1/32°

les reproductions les plus parfaites dans le monde du jouet

avec l'autorisation expresse des grands Constructeurs

In the 1950s, sheets of blotting paper ('buvards') carrying advertisements were a popular means of advertising in France. This one shows the first ten cars in the Minialuxe range, together with various accessories.

production, but soon after, it seems, the Minialuxe brand disappeared. Among the last cars to be modelled were the Renault 30TS and the Volkswagen K70.

Over the previous twenty years, Minialuxe may have won some battles, but it was Norev that won the war.

Norev and Minialuxe dominated this sector of the toy market in France, but there was a host of smaller entries into the field too. The remainder of this chapter summarises a few of the more interesting ones.

Clé

Not far away from the Minialuxe factory, in the Quartier Gouilloux, Oyonnax, were the premises of Monsieur Clément Gaget who used the first three letters of his name as a trade name, Clé. The word 'clef' in French means key, providing an easily recognisable logo.

Clé originally made plastic novelties, key rings and kitchenware and then branched into toy cars aimed firmly at the cheaper end of the market. What made Clé distinctive was that many of its cars were offered in three sizes: 1/64, 1/48 and 1/32 scale. The larger cars came with or without friction motors. While Clé did not seem to sell its cars in individual boxes, some were sold in bubble-pack packaging and the 1/64 scale ones have been seen packed in threes on a backing card. Later on, Clé made the 'Belle Epoque' series of veteran and vintage cars and these were individually boxed. Clé seems to have disappeared from the scene in the early 1970s.

BS

Beuzen et Sordet (BS) was another minor plastic car manufacturer. Like Clé, it made simple cars in different scales (1/43 and 1/33), but the quality of moulding was noticeably superior, particularly in the case of the larger models. Like some Minialuxe products, BS cars sometimes came in boxes marked 'Punch'. All were representations of popular French cars of the time: the Citroën 2CV, Peugeot 403, Simca Versailles and Renault Floride were to 1/33 scale, and the Panhard Dyna Z, Peugeot 403, Citroën DS, Simca Aronde and Ariane came in 1/43 scale. The most sought-after BS product was a Citroën H van with a rear section in the shape of a cooker, a promotion for Sougland kitchen appliances. Production of BS cars ceased around 1962.

Injectaplastic

This little-known firm was active in the early 1970s and made a few racing and vintage cars that are of little interest. By contrast, its four 1/43 cars, Simca 1100, Renault R16 and – particularly – Peugeot 204 coupé and Citroën DS21, are very desirable, as are the Citroën DS and CX estate cars made to 1/33 scale and issued in Police, Ambulance and Fire liveries. The Injectaplastic cars were not invidually boxed but came in 'blister' packs.

GéGé

Another trademark formed from the founder's name: Germain Giroud, whose initials would in French be pronounced 'GéGé'. Already well-known for making dolls and other toys, the company brought out its first plastic cars in 1954, a series of exceptionally well-finished electrically-driven models in 1/20 scale. The range comprised a Renault Frégate and Ford Vedette (and Vendome, the top-of-the-range luxury model), with a Peugeot 203 and Simca Aronde being added in 1955 and a Simca Versailles/Ariane and Citroën DS 19 the following year. Sadly, most surviving examples of these models suffer badly from warping.

In 1956-57, GéGé ventured into the 1/43 field, with scaled-down versions of the same cars. Unusually, these had diecast bases with friction motors but GéGé still managed to fit front seats and a steering wheel inside – features that were not to become standard practice on diecast models for some years yet. These were also sold in self-assembly form, which is why the baseplate is screwed on rather than riveted. Fortunately, the smaller cars retain their shape much better than their bigger brothers. The only problem is that they hardly ever surface on the collectors' market now …

JEP

JEP (Jouets de Paris) was one of the biggest and longest-established French toy companies, with decades of experience of making tin toys dating as far back as 1902. However, JEP's role in the development of plastic cars was a comparatively small one. In 1958, a group of five French cars appeared – Citroën DS, Peugeot 403, Simca Versailles, Peugeot 403 and Renault Dauphine. The inspiration may have come from the GéGé range: with the exception of the Dauphine, they were the same subjects and, like the GéGés, were similarly constructed with a die-cast chassis and plastic bodyshell. This lack of originality may be why the JEPs made little impact at the time.

By contrast, JEP's packaging was extremely imaginative, taking the form of a box that opens out to create a scenic background. Only the Dauphine came in a conventional style of box carton.

Between 1957 and 1960, JEP made four larger cars between 21 and 30cm in length – a Simca Aronde, Citroën DS, Panhard Dyna

LA "DS 19" CITROEN

Elle est conforme en tout point à la véritable " DS 19 ", dernier modèle de " CITROEN " • Carrosserie en trois teintes • Carlingue entièrement chromée • Réduction fidèle à l'échelle 1/12ème • Phares éclairants • Moteur électrique.

VOITURES ÉLECTRIQUES

Tellement plus belles les voitures GÉGÉ

GéGé

CHEZ TOUS LES MARCHANDS DE JOUETS
4

PUB. « Édition des Revues de France »

The GéGé Citroën DS 19 was advertised in the French edition of Meccano *magazine in January 1957.*

and Peugeot 404 – which could be friction-driven or controlled via a steering wheel and rods inserted through the rear window (téléguidée). Almost as an afterthought, JEP produced one more plastic car before going out of business in 1968, and it turned out to be the company's best effort in this genre: a hugely desirable Citroën DS convertible, perfectly proportioned, well-finished … and impossible to find today.

Vapé-Bourbon

As the double-barrelled name suggests, this was really two separate firms: Vapé is a contraction of Vanotti et Perinetti, who made plastic toys, while Bourbon distributed them and negotiated promotional deals, notably with Poclain, who manufactured road building machinery such as excavators. In addition, the Vapé-Bourbon range consisted of Peugeot D4 and J7 delivery vans, available in many

ÉCOLE DE CONDUITE

JEP

APPRENEZ A CONDUIRE AVEC LES AUTOS TÉLÉGUIDÉES JEP

JEP vous propose trois voitures automobiles véritables maquettes en réduction au 1/15e des
SIMCA ARONDE
DYNA PANHARD
et au 1/20e de la Citroën DS 19.

Ce sont des modèles réduits strictement à l'échelle avec tous les détails des vraies voitures :

Les carrosseries sont en matière moulée incassable et teintée dans la masse aux couleurs des constructeurs.

Elles sont munies de glaces et de pare-brise.

Les pare-chocs et calandres sont en métal fondu sous pression.

Roues de luxe avec pneus et montées sur ressorts.

Un volant en matière moulée avec tiges de commande démontables permet la conduite facile à distance de la voiture. Toutes les manœuvres sont possibles. Dispositif breveté.

Nº 2675. — Aronde conduite à distance. Long. 26 cm.

Nº 2685. — Panhard 59 conduite à distance. Long. 30 cm.

Nº 2374. — Citroën DS 19, conduite à distance, malle ouvrante. Long. 22 cm.

Nº 7675. — Aronde avec mouvement d'horlogerie et levier de marche et arrêt.

Nº 7685. — Dyna-Panhard avec mouvement d'horlogerie et levier de marche et arrêt.

Nº 2274. — Avec petit volant de direction pour jouer sur une table.

— 35 —

Best known for its model railways, JEP also made these 1/15 and 1/20 scale cars which could be operated by an ingenious remote-control steering wheel.

different promotional liveries, and Berliet trucks and petrol tankers. The best of the bunch is the imposing articulated Berliet GAK tanker, which comes in six different petrol liveries: BP, Total, Mobil, Elf, Esso and Shell.

Sésame

Sésame was based at 70 rue de la Poyat, Saint-Claude, in the Jura region. Although its toy vehicles were still on sale in the early 1970s, they hark back to an earlier era with their combination of a simple plastic body and colourful lithographed tin, recalling the British Wells-Brimtoys of the early fifties. A handful of delivery vans – Citroën 2CV, Renault 4 and Renault Estafette – and a few articulated truck cabs based on Simca, Mercedes, Berliet and Bernard prototypes served as the basis of a vast range of different advertising liveries. Sésame also made a few cars which, if anything, were even simpler in style: a Simca 1500, Ford Taunus, Citroën Ami, Renault 4L and R8, Simca 1000 and a Peugeot 404 coupé.

Sésame toys tended to be sold cheaply on market stalls rather than in toy shops, and collectors captivated by their Gallic charm can still pick them up at modest prices today – in France at least.

France Jouets

Known by the initials FJ, this firm began making tin toys in 1954 in its factory on the Avenue de la Capelette in Marseilles. Best known for a series of 1/50 scale diecast Berliet and GMC trucks, FJ also made excellent larger plastic vehicles such as a Citroën DS (8.25 inches long), Peugeot 404 (8 inches) and a very impressive Renault Estafette (11 inches), available in white in 'Secours Routier' livery. Most sought-after of all is the Estafette pick-up in Coca-Cola livery, complete with crates of bottles. All of these were powered by electric motors and operated via a control box.

FRANCE

Norev Simca Aronde ▶

The first 1/43 plastic Norev car, a Simca Aronde, appeared in 1953. The earliest issues can be identified by their shiny metal base, later painted black. First generation Norev cars carried a paper tag informing the buyer that they were made from 'Rhodialite', a plastic composition developed by Rhone-Poulenc.
Price guide: £35

◀ Norev Renault 4CV

The rear-engined Renault 4CV was unveiled at the Paris Motor Show in 1946 and proved so popular that over a million were built over the next fifteen years. As such, it was a natural subject for Norev to choose to model. The white tyres and red hubs on this version indicate that it dates from around 1955.
Price guide: £35

Norev Renault 4CV ▶

Many colour and wheel variations can be found on the 4CV. This is a later issue with black tyres and plated wheel hubs, fitted from 1961 onwards.
Price guide: £35

Ford Vedette
Originally intended for production in the United States as a 'compact' car, the Vedette was assembled in Ford's French plant and was unusual at the time in having a V8 engine. This was no.2 in Norev's 1/43 scale series.
Price guide: £35

Norev Peugeot 203 ▶
The white tyres identify this as another early Norev issue. Most of the early cars were fitted with a radio aerial and many came in both freewheeling and friction drive versions.
Price guide: £30

Citroën DS
The futuristic lines of the DS caused a sensation when it was announced in 1955. This was the first Norev model to feature window glazing. Note the box style of early Norevs, which was designed to look like a wooden packing case.
Price guide: £30

Citroën DS ▶

The real Citroën had a separate roof panel made of plastic – just like the Norev version! A common fault on early Norevs is for a chemical reaction to take place where two plastic sections join, causing discolouration as on this example.
Price guide: £30

▲
Norev Renault Dauphine

Like the 4CV which it eventually replaced, the 1956 Dauphine had a rear-mounted engine. Norev was good at coming up with novel ways of promoting its products and the background to this picture shows a paper bag depicting models from the Norev range which was supplied to toy shops.
Price guide: £25

▲
Norev Lancia Aurelia

While most Norev cars were French, some were chosen from further afield, such as this stylish Lancia Aurelia coupé.
Price guide: £25

◀ **Norev Panhard Dyna with skis**

Powered by an air-cooled engine of only 850cc, the 1954 Panhard Dyna was nevertheless a full six-seater. This version of the Norev with roof rack and skis is much rarer than the ordinary issue, as such small accessories are very easily lost.
Price guide: £60

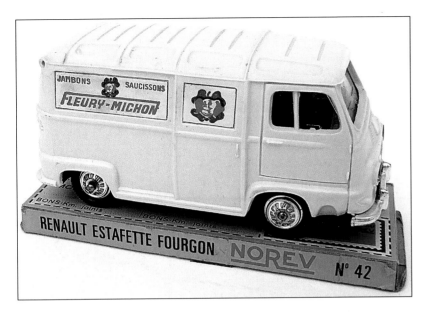

Norev Renault Estafette van

The Norev model of the Renault Estafette delivery van appeared in 1961 and featured rear doors which opened in three sections, as on the real thing. Numerous different liveries were available, such as Fleury Michon, a maker of meat products. The advertisements are simply paper stickers.
Price guide: £25

Norev Renault 4 van

Norev added the smaller R4 van to its range in 1963, featuring opening side and rear doors. The turquoise van is in the livery of 'Cibié', a French maker of car headlights while 'Locatel' was a television rental company. Other liveries available included Amora Mustard, Hoover and Calor, in addition to several rare issues done as special promotionals.
Price guide: £30

Norev Land Rover Expedition

This Land Rover short wheelbase station wagon dates from 1969 and is one of the more sought-after Norev models in the UK, on account of the popularity of the prototype. Variations include a Gendarmerie model with roof light and aerial, a breakdown truck, and a pick-up with canvas cover and trailer. There were also military versions, both short and long wheelbase, fitted with trailers, figures and weaponry.
Price guide: £65

Minialuxe Simca Aronde ▶

Soon after Norev launched its 1/43 series, Minialuxe entered the same market. Minialuxe's Simca Aronde is clearly less successful in capturing the lines of the real car. To the collector today, however, it appeals because of its simple period charm and because of the attractive box artwork.
Price guide: £40

Minialuxe Hotchkiss Grégoire
Minialuxe was the only mainstream toy manufacturer to model this obscure car. The Grégoire was an innovative design with a flat-four light alloy engine mounted ahead of the wheels, enclosed in a bodyshell which, by 1950s standards, was exceptionally aerodynamic. Its high price meant that the car secured a mere 248 buyers. The Minialuxe can also be found as a taxi, and with a roof rack and luggage.
Price guide: £50

Minialuxe Renault Dauphine ▶
Another popular French car modelled by both Norev and Minialuxe. The same generic box was used for all the early Minialuxe cars, the name of the vehicle inside being stamped on the end flap.
Price guide: £40

◀ Minialuxe Citroën DS
Practically every French range of model cars included a replica of the Citroën DS, and Minialuxe is no exception. This is the earliest version, with solid white wheels and no window glazing. Later, a transparent upper section was fitted, combining roof and windows. Minialuxe also issued the car as a convertible, simply removing the top section and creating a four-door cabriolet which never actually existed!
Price guide: £40

Minialuxe Citroën Traction Avant ▶

In the late 1960s, Minialuxe reused an earlier mould, bringing it up-to-date by fitting window glazing, seats and plated parts. The backing card shows a caricature drawing of the Belgian writer Georges Simenon's famous detective, Maigret, standing outside the Quai des Orfèvres in Paris, where the headquarters of the police judiciaire are situated.
Price guide: £30

Minialuxe Simca 1000 Police Car

Model car makers have always been fond of making police cars and taxis, for the simple reason that this allows them to use the same mould to produce several different versions. In France, police patrol cars were nicknamed voiture pie (magpie) on account of their black and white markings.
Price guide: £20

Minialuxe Simca Plein Ciel ▶

This elegant car was known as the Océane in convertible form and Plein Ciel as a coupé. The radiator grille is that of the 1958 model.
Price guide: £40

Minialuxe Peugeot 403 ▶

The 403 was in production from 1955 to 1966, and was a reliable workhorse. The look of the Minialuxe model is improved by window glazing.
Price guide: £40

Minialuxe Ford Anglia ◀

The Anglia 105E is one of two British Fords modelled by Minialuxe, the other being the Consul Classic. Again, the body is moulded in two parts. On most surviving models, the plated wheels have started to split.
Price guide: £35

Minialuxe Peugeot 404 ▶

Introduced in 1960, the Pininfarina-designed 404 was envisaged as a successor to the 403, which nevertheless remained in production for a further six years. As with the Citroën DS, Minialuxe turned this model into a four-door convertible by removing the roof, though no such car existed in real life.
Price guide: £30

Minialuxe Citroën Ami ◀

Over one million of these unusual-looking cars were made between 1961 and 1969. Moulding the body in two sections allowed Minialuxe to create bright two-tone combinations.
Price guide: £45

Minialuxe Ford Taunus
This 1960 German Ford had clean, aerodynamic lines. Note that Minialuxe cars of this period were now supplied in individually designed picture boxes.
Price guide: £35 ◀

Minialuxe BMW 1500 ▶
In the later 1960s, Perspex display cases replaced cardboard boxes. Minialuxe was fond of fitting different accessories such as luggage racks or this canoe.
Price guide: £20

Minialuxe Jaguar E-type
By the late 1960s, Minialuxe quality had improved dramatically compared to earlier issues, though this was not enough to save the company. The E Type also comes as a convertible.
Price guide: £40 ◀

Minialuxe Paris Bus ▶
This Paris bus is based on a Somua prototype, in service from 1955 onwards. The Minialuxe model was a very popular line in Paris souvenir shops.
Price guide: £60

FRANCE

Minialuxe Renault Estafette Taxi Camionnette
Unlike the rival Norev company, Minialuxe also made many models in 1/32 scale. This Estafette van has very fragile opening rear doors, often missing on non-mint examples.
Price guide: £35

Minialuxe Citroën DS 19 ▶
The Simca P60 and the Citroën DS 19 were the first two cars modelled in 1/32 scale by Minialuxe. Window glazing is achieved by moulding the upper half of the body in clear plastic and then painting the roof section. The car is powered by a friction motor.
Price guide: £75

Minialuxe Simca Versailles
This car was developed as a successor to the Ford Vedette, but by the time it went on sale in 1955, Ford of France had merged with Simca. The boot on the Minialuxe model opens, an unusual feature for the period.
Price guide: £75

▼

▲

Minialuxe Simca Marly Ambulance
The estate car version of the Versailles was known as the Marly and was modelled by Minialuxe as an ambulance, complete with stretcher inside. A very fragile item fitted with various accessories, the ambulance would not have lasted long in a child's hands.
Price guide: £75

Minialuxe Renault Dauphine ▶
Minialuxe brought out this 1/32 version of the Dauphine in September 1956. It not only has an opening front luggage compartment but a hinged tray underneath for the spare wheel. This is a rare version with a 1958 Monte Carlo rally sticker.
Price guide: £100

◀ **Minialuxe Simca Beaulieu**
This Simca Beaulieu appeared in 1958 and reflects American styling trends of the period. The Minialuxe model features an opening boot and plated accessories.
Price guide: £75

Minialuxe Petrol Pump set
Minialuxe took a great deal of trouble over packaging design, giving even a simple petrol pump set an attractive picture box.
Price guide: £40
▼

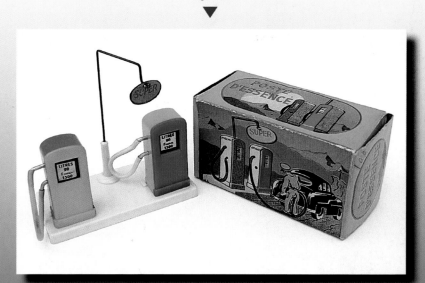

▲
Minialuxe Peugeot 604 Tour de France
A late Minialuxe issue from the early 1970s, sold to coincide with the annual Tour de France cycle race.
Price guide: £30

Mont Blanc 'Le Petit Garagiste' set ▶

Jouets Mont Blanc was a trademark registered by Joseph Vuillerme in 1947 for his toy products made in the town of Romilly, in the Haute-Savoie region. Mont Blanc made toy vehicles, particularly some impressive Berliet trucks, first in tin and later in plastic. This set contains two seven inch-long American-style station wagons with interchangeable bodies and chassis. A very similar model was made in the USA by Precision Plastics Co from 1948 onwards, and the Mont Blanc may have been made under licence. The set was announced to the French toy trade in 1953.
Price guide: £75

— Marque Déposée —
« JOUETS MONT-BLANC »

FABRICATION FRANÇAISE MARQUE DÉPOSÉE

JOUETS MONT-BLANC

VENTE EN GROS

Henri VERPIOT & CI. MAMEAUX

SALLES D'EXPOSITION

36, rue du Mont-Thabor   24, rue Rabelais
PARIS (1er)   **LYON** (3e)

Manufacture de Jouets Mécaniques

J. VULLIERME, à **RUMILLY** (Haute-Savoie)

Téléphone : 188

NOUVEAUTÉS

TRACTEUR A CHENILLES "MONT-BLANC" avec sa remorque

Mécanisme breveté S.G.D.G. lui permettant de tourner à droite et à gauche. Carrosserie plastique 2 couleurs. Mécanique puissante.

Dimensions : 190 mm. x 100 mm. — Hauteur 100 mm.

LE PETIT GARAGISTE

Auto démontable en boîte-présentation contenant chassis, moteur, roues et 2 carrosseries.

AUTRES NOUVEAUTÉS :

LA TOUPIE LUMINEUSE

LE STYL'O — LOUFOC'AUTO — LA SIRÈNE — LE BABY-TRAIN — L'ÉLÉVATEUR DE CONSTRUCTION — L'AUTOGYRE — LES PISTOLETS — LA SOUCOUPE VOLANTE — LA TOUPIE DIABOLIQUE — LE TURBORÉACTEUR - ETC...

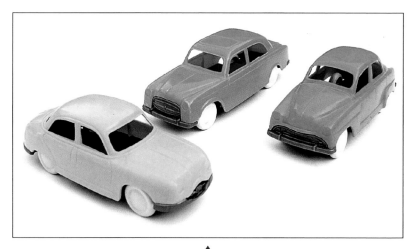

Les Rouliers Renault 'Etoile Filante'

Les Rouliers was an obscure company which made a range of Matchbox-sized diecast trucks, but this seems to be its only 1/43 scale plastic car. The Etoile Filante ('Shooting Star') was a one-off gas turbine car which reached a record speed of 308.9 km/h at Bonneville Salt Flats in 1956.
Price guide: £20

BS Simca Versailles

Another from the BS 1/32 series. More realistic than the smaller BS cars, these were moulded in good quality plastic that does not become misshapen over time.
Price guide: £20 (unboxed)

BS 1/43 scale cars

BS made simple, brightly-coloured plastic cars in around 1/43 scale, based on popular French vehicles of the mid-1950s. Shown here are (left to right) Panhard Dyna, Peugeot 403 and Simca Aronde.
Price guide: £10 each

BS Renault Floride

The Floride, designed in Italy by Frua, looked elegant and sporty but was basically a Renault Dauphine underneath. This 1/32 model was made by BS but distributed under the name 'Punch'. The box was printed in different colours according to the finish of the toy inside.
Price guide: £80

FRANCE

BS Peugeot 403 ▶

This 1/32 scale version of the 403 is considerably more realistic than the same manufacturer's 1/43 scale one.
Price guide: £20 (unboxed)

Bourbon Berliet GAK Tanker 'Elf' ◀

Bourbon offered this Berliet articulated tanker in the liveries of numerous petrol companies active in France in the mid-1960s. Elf (Essence et Lubrifiants de France) was formed in 1967 by regrouping a number of other petrol brands.
Price guide: £75

Bourbon Berliet GAK Tanker 'Total' ▶

Another variation on the Berliet tanker, in the livery of Total, a French petrol brand founded in 1954. Bourbon also made a Berliet tanker on a shorter, non-articulated, chassis.
Price guide: £75

JEP Panhard Dyna ◀

Although the subjects chosen were similar, the difference between JEP and the likes of Norev or Minialuxe was that the JEPs had plastic bodies and a heavy diecast base. The Dyna also comes in dark blue. The box is the most attractive feature of the toy.
Price guide: £75

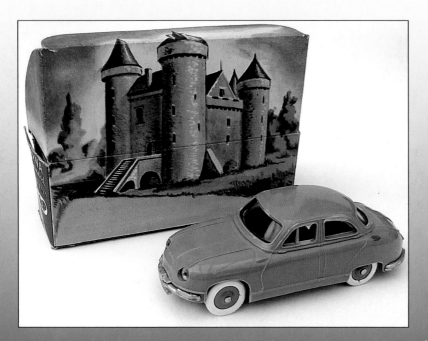

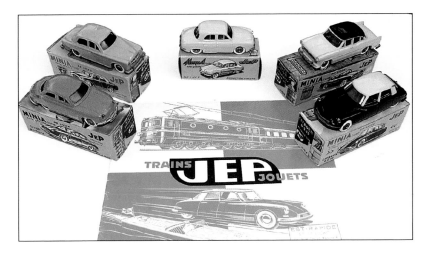

JEP Group
The five JEP cars: (left to right), Panhard, Peugeot, Renault, Simca and Citroën, pictured with a JEP catalogue. The vast majority of JEP toys consisted of trains.
Price guide: £75 each

Sésame Simca Tanker 'Caltex' ▶
Sésame toys combined traditional lithographed tinplate with a plastic body. Models came with or without friction motors. The articulated tankers and trucks appear to be the only models to have individual boxes.
Price guide: £30

JEP Peugeot 403
Although not very well proportioned – the bonnet looks too long – the JEP Peugeot also comes with a very stylish box which opens out into a replica of a Peugeot garage.
Price guide: £75

JEP Renault Dauphine ▶
The Dauphine is the only one of the five JEP 1/43 scale cars that comes in a conventional carton-style of box, rather than a more elaborate display one.
Price guide: £75

Sésame Renault Estafette Van 'Midica'
These vans were generally packed in trade boxes of twenty pieces. The 'Midica' van is unusual as the lettering is done by means of a waterslide transfer rather than lithographed tin. A huge number of different liveries appeared on this van.
Price guide: £15

Sésame Bernard Van 'Magdeleine' ▶
The Bernard cab unit also comes with articulated trailers, as do the Mercedes, Berliet GAK, Berliet Stradair and Simca. 'Magdeleine' is a brand of biscuits.
Price guide: £15

◀ **Sésame Renault 4**
One of only seven cars in the Sésame range. Lacking the colourful advertising of the vans, the cars are very simple and basic designs.
Price guide: £8

Sésame Gift Set ▶
A gift set (coffret in French) such as this is worth more than the sum of its parts. A similar military set also exists.
Price guide: £100

GéGé Simca Versailles ▶

This elaborate model is quite a contrast to the simple Sésames. 9.5 inches in length, it comes with a battery-controller in the form of a miniature dashboard, complete with a steering wheel to change the car's direction. On the licence plate, 5450 GG 42, the final two digits represent the département of the Loire, where the toys were made in a factory at Montbrison.
Price guide: £100+

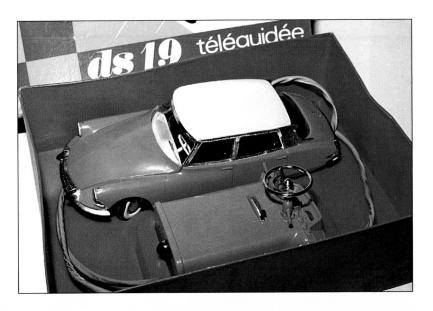

◀ **GéGé Citroën DS 19**
The Citroën DS was the favourite car of all French toy manufacturers, and it is no surprise to find it in the GéGé 1/20th series. This dark pink shade is one of the less common variations. This is the remote control (téléguidée) version; the car also came with a battery compartment underneath and an on/off switch at the rear.
Price guide: £100+
(Courtesy Bruce Sterling)

FJ Peugeot 404 ▶

An 8 inch-long replica of the Peugeot 404 with a space underneath for batteries. The France Jouets (FJ) catalogue also shows a 404 rally car and police car.
Price guide: £50

◀ **Clé set of three 1/64 scale cars**
Various combinations of models were sold in sets of three on a backing card representing parking spaces on the Rue de Rivoli, Paris. Left to right: Citroën Traction Avant, Citroën DS, Panhard Dyna.
Price guide: £30

FRANCE

Clé Citroën 2CV van ▶
The 1/48 scale Citroën looks better in this Cibié livery than in the more usual plain grey version. It is rare to find separately packed Clé models.
Price guide: £25

◀ Clé Simca Oceane sports
The most attractive models in the 1/48 series are the earlier issues with white tyres.
Price guide: £10

Clé Citroën Traction Avant ▶
One of the 1/32 scale series, with chrome-plated bumpers and roof aerial.
Price guide: £20

◀ Clé Citroën DS 19
Another model from the 1/32 scale series. These are more cheaply finished than Minialuxe's cars in a similar size, lacking separate bumpers, lights, etc.
Price guide: £20

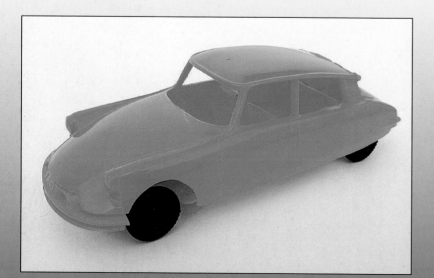

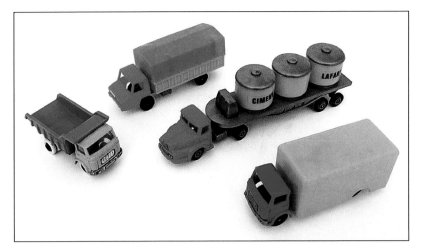

Clé trucks
Clé made a large number of variations on the Berliet GAK, Stradair and Unic chassis. These are relatively common, but there are a few special promotional models that can fetch much higher prices.
Price guide: £7 each

Clé 1930 Packard
The Matchbox 'Models of Yesteryear' series started a trend towards vintage cars which many other manufacturers followed, and Clé was no exception. The 'Belle Epoque' series came in more elaborate packaging than other Clé products.
Price guide: £5

Cofalu Police Motorcycles
Cofalu, mainly known for its metal figures and roadside accessories, also made some plastic toys.
Price guide: £10 each

Cofalu Tour de France set
Many Cofalu toys were associated with the Tour de France bicycle race. The Peugeot 404 is a very simple likeness, but considerable effort has gone into the presentation of the set.
Price guide: £60

Injectaplastic Citroën DS
This little-known range contained just four 1/43 scale cars: Peugeot 204 coupé, Simca 1100, Renault R16, and this Citroën DS21 which features the face-lifted front of post-1968 models.
Price guide: £25

Injectaplastic Citroën DS21 PTT ▶
There were two other Injectaplastic Citroëns, based on estate car versions of the DS21 and the later CX models. Each of these came in fire, ambulance, police, Gendarmerie and Post (PTT) liveries. These are all to a larger – c.1/33 – scale.
Price guide: £25

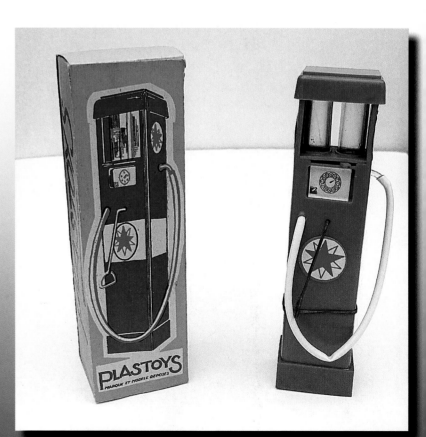

▲
Plastica Renault Frégate
Yet another obscure French plastic maker. Although crude by the standards of Norev or Minialuxe, Plastica's cars, in approximately 1/40-1/43 scale, did include some unusual subjects like a Delahaye and a Ford Comète coupé.
Price guide: £10

Plastoys Azur Petrol Pump ▶
A 6.75 inch replica of a petrol pump in Azur livery. It can be filled with water which can then be pumped out by moving the lever backwards and forwards. Plastoys is also known to have made some simple plastic trucks.
Price guide: £20

SLJ Citroën Ami ▶

A 7.5 inch (1/20 scale) friction-driven car which is finished to a high standard, featuring correctly styled wheel trims, and even seats with imitation cloth effect.
Price guide: £50

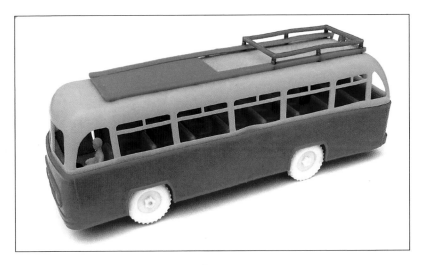

▲
Robot Coach

This 10 inch polythene coach is marked 'made in France' underneath and carries the word 'Robot' on the roof – perhaps the maker's name. This is a simple but attractive toy, based on a Mercedes prototype. There is a roof ladder at the rear and a sliding roof panel.
Price guide: £10

Unknown Berliet Stradair ▶

Most soft plastic toys tended to be quite large, but this four inch Berliet Stradair is in approximately 1/50th scale.
Price guide: £6

◀ **Unknown Renault Etoile Filante**
Another 'soft' plastic toy, representing Renault's 1956 gas-turbine record car. Seven inches in length, it carries no identification marks.
Price guide: £15

SPAIN

Although it is not very far from the beaches of the Costa Blanca, few holidaymakers are likely to make the trip inland to the industrial town of Ibi, Alicante, which has been the centre of the Spanish toy industry for more than 100 years.

History shows that toy manufacture often evolves out of the production of something else. A case in point is Paya, Spain's longest-established toy company which was founded in 1905. At the end of the nineteenth century, a major industry in Ibi was the transportation of ice from the surrounding hills for use in the coastal fish markets. A by-product was the manufacture of ice cream, for which metal containers were required. These were supplied by a family of tinsmiths by the name of Paya which, as a sideline, also made miniature household items for use as children's toys.

One of the Paya brothers, Raimondo, started to buy examples of tin toys, which in these days mostly came from Germany. He used to buy two of each, one to dismantle in order to study the mechanism, and one to keep. Today, many of these tin toys can be seen in the Valencian Toy Museum at Ibi, where the history of the early days of Paya is well-documented.

As in any other industry, competition soon emerged. In 1910, some Paya employees decided to go it alone and set up Verdù y Cia, later joining with Santiago Rico Molina, a doll manufacturer, to form a new company in 1922: Rico SA (Sociedad Anónima). No doubt taking inspiration from this, some more ex-Paya personnel decided to set up a similar venture and founded González and Company, later known as Picó and Company after Manuel Picó. In 1936, Picó founded Juguetes y Estuches SA, using the initials JYE and Jyesa as trademarks.

Thus, by the early 1930s, Ibi had developed into a thriving centre of tin toy manufacture with three companies – Paya, Rico and Jyesa – competing against each other with similar products. This golden age of Spanish toy production was short-lived. All of Europe's toy industry suffered during the Second World War, but in the case of Spain the decline set in earlier as a result of the Civil War which broke out in 1936. It wasn't until the 1950s that toy manufacture picked up again, by which time, tinplate was gradually being replaced by plastic – not that this marked a decline in quality: Paya, Rico and Jyesa quickly

Paya's 'Construccione' series consisted of interchangeable plastic body components mounted on a common chassis.

781 SEDAN 4 PUERTAS

782 RUBIA

787 CABRIOLÉ

790 ROADSTER

793 FURGONETA REPARTO

794 FURGONETA SANIDAD

PROYECCIÓN

UTILLAJE

TRATAMIENTO TERMICO

mastered the transition from tin pressing to injection moulding and produced what are arguably the best and more realistic plastic cars ever made, mostly in scales ranging from 1/32 to 1/18.

It seems that these toys were largely produced for the home market, so that few of them surface here, making them all the more elusive for British collectors.

Paya

Paya's first venture into plastic was the 'Construcciones' series of 1954. These came in sets with a tinplate chassis and clockwork motor, with a variety of bodies in plastic. All have a similar, American-style grille, vaguely inspired by Buicks of the period. Though ingeniously designed, they are not scale models as such, as they aren't based on exact prototypes.

The next series, in 1/32 scale, represented a significant step forward in terms of realism. Based on the same constructional principle, though now fitted with friction rather than clockwork mechanisms, this range of contemporary European cars was sold in both kit and completely built form. There were many desirable subjects from France (Simca Versailles, Citroën DS, Renault 4CV, Dauphine and Simca Elysée), Germany (Mercedes 300 SL Roadster, Mercedes 220S, Volkswagen, Borgward Isabella, Opel Rekord and Porsche 356), plus an Alfa Romeo Giulietta sports car and a Studebaker Lark. All of these are rare, with the DS Citroën, as so often, being highly sought-after in Europe.

The Citroën, it seems, was just as popular in Spain as in France, and the futuristic shape of the DS gained it the nickname 'Tiburon', which means 'Shark' in Spanish. Paya made several models of it, one of them being as large as 1/12 scale. This magnificent item was battery-driven by means of a remote-control box, which could also operate the lights and horn. At the other extreme in terms of size, Paya made a few 1/43 scale models which are equally rare. The Renault 4CV is copied from Norev's plastic model, while the Volkswagen van (also available as a microbus, pick-up and a 'Gasolina' tanker) is very closely based on a diecast from the Danish firm of Tekno. Both the Renault and VW share the same box, with pictures of the car, van and microbus being shown on different sides. The Renault is freewheeling but the VW van contains a simple friction mechanism.

Irrespective of scale, there was one make of car that Paya favoured more than any other, and that was Spain's first mass-produced car, the SEAT. Prior to the Second World War, Spanish drivers relied entirely on imported vehicles, as the only cars built in Spain were costly and exclusive like the Hispano-Suiza. In fact, Spain was well behind other European countries in terms of industrial development – deliberately so, as General Franco, the victor of the Civil War, was opposed to industrial modernisation which he believed would turn a 'people of peasants and conquistadors into a society plagued by materialism'.

Mass motoring finally became a prospect after 1953, when Fiat signed a deal with the Spanish government to set up an assembly plant in the Industrial Zone of Barcelona to assemble the 1400A model. The name SEAT was adopted, an acronym for 'Sociedad Espanola de Automoviles de Turismo' – which basically doesn't mean

anything more than 'Spanish car company'. At last Spain had its own mass-produced car – but it was hardly an affordable 'people's car'. That eventually came along when production of the 600 model began in 1957. In 1959, the rounded shape of the 1400 saloon gave way to the sharper lines of the 1400C, a smaller-engined version of the Fiat 1800/2100 model. Before long, Spanish roads were full of Seats and, inevitably, Spanish toy shops were full of models of them. Starting with the 1400A, Paya systematically modelled each new SEAT car, in numerous scales and often in multiple taxi, police and ambulance versions.

As a postscript, it's worth mentioning that Paya continued to make toy vehicles of one kind or another until well into the 1980s, though the level of realism achieved in plastic in the 1960s was never surpassed.

Rico

The products of Rico, the rival company set up by some ex-Paya employees in 1922, were very similar to Paya, starting with tin toys and moving into plastic in the 1950s. One particular characteristic of Rico's plastic cars is that they tend not to be moulded in their final colour, but are spray-painted like diecasts so that they don't really look as if they're plastic at all. While Rico made a vast number of large-scale cars, its most interesting series was in a scale of around 1/38-1/40, making them smaller than similar Paya cars but slightly bigger than regular 1/43 size diecasts.

Again, like Paya, Rico made many models of SEAT cars. The 1400C saloon was a particular favourite, in taxi, police, estate car and ambulance guises. Though never imported into the UK, the 1400C looks quite familiar to British eyes, partly because it was designed by Pininfarina whose style can be recognised in the Austin Cambridge and other BMC cars of the period. A more exotic and much less frequently modelled Spanish car, was the Pegaso, designed by an engineer from Barcelona by the name of Wilfredo Pelayo Ricart. Between 1951 and 1957, only 85 Pegasos were made, and a third of these are believed to have survived. One of the most sought-after Rico models is the Pegaso Z-103 sports which, like all such convertibles, rarely survives with the fragile windscreen intact.

After this brief foray into performance car production, Pegaso concentrated on the more mundane business of catering for Spain's commercial vehicle needs. Pegaso trucks had quite a stylish cab design nonetheless, and Rico produced several of these. Another popular commercial vehicle in Spain was the DKW van, as the German firm assembled these in a factory in the Basque region. A sloping-fronted 1957 DKW van can be found in the Rico range, as well as the later 1960 Auto Union F 1000 L, available in fire, ambulance, school bus and 'television' liveries. Among other Rico models in the same scale are an Opel Kapitan, three Renaults (the 4CV, Dauphine and R4) and, of particular interest to British collectors, a short-wheelbase Land Rover.

All of these models are powered – if that is the right word – by a simple metal flywheel which barely propels the car more than a few inches! That may be one reason why the range didn't remain in production all that long – probably between 1958 and 1967, the last

Nacoral's Chiqui Cars were made of plastic in 1/43 scale. Some were later issued with diecast metal bodies.

addition being an American car, a 1966 Dodge Dart, which Rico also made as a large battery-operated model. Like Paya, Rico continued to make bigger plastic toy cars until production ceased in 1984.

Plastic cars have been made in many countries, but the finish and detailing of those made in Spain in the 1960s are of a particularly high quality, though they did become more toy-like in the seventies. While Paya and Rico were the big names in this field, several other firms made similar products – Vercor, Comando, Roman, Plasticos Albacete, Nacoral, Karpan and Gozan being a few of the other trademarks about which little is known outside Spain.

Anguplas

One other Spanish plastic range deserves a mention here: Anguplas, a series of 1/86 scale models dating from between 1958-1966. This was a vast range, encompassing not just miniature cars, but 'Plastilandia' building kits,

obviously suitable as accessories for HO scale railway layouts. As so often, the makers were already involved in something else, in this case the production of plastic household utensils. Anguplas made a good selection of European and American cars of the period, with subjects as diverse as Land Rovers, an Edsel, a Studebaker Lark, a Ford Anglia and numerous Pegaso and Ford Thames trucks (the latter being called Ebro in Spain). Anguplas models in good condition are hard to find today as the type of plastic used means that most survivors have become misshapen. Later, some of the moulds were reissued under the Eko name and supplies of these were distributed in the UK during the 1980s.

Today, a century after the Paya brothers started making tin toys, Ibi remains a thriving centre of toy production. A Spanish trade guide lists as many as 490 companies currently involved in the production, distribution and sale of toys in the Alicante area. An indication of just how important toys ('juguetes' in Spanish) are in this part of Spain can be gauged from the name of one of Ibi's streets: Avenida del Juguete!

www.velocebooks.com/www.veloce.co.uk
All current books • New book news • Special offers • Gift vouchers

Comando: Mercedes 'Policia' ▶

The box identifies this police car as part of the 'Comando' series, a product of Juguetes Joaquin Valero, based in Ibi, Alicante. Powered by a friction motor, the Mercedes also comes as a black/yellow Barcelona taxi. Length: 6 inches.
Price guide: £30

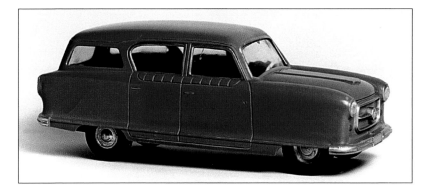

JYE Nash Rambler

Partly-covered wheelarches were a characteristic of Nash styling in the early 1950s, giving rise to nicknames such as the 'bathtub' look. This friction-driven estate car is about 9.25 inches long. The maker's logo, JYE, appears on the tinplate base and also on the centre of the grille.
Price guide: £75
(Courtesy Alex J. Cameron)

JYE Volkswagen Microbus ▶

Another high quality model from JYE, made from a type of plastic that does not warp – a common problem with early plastic models. Length: 6.75 inches.
Price guide: £100

Cayro Citroën Barcelona Taxi

This rare 1/43 scale Citroën Traction Avant is the one and only model attributable to Cayro, which was based in Denia, near Valencia. The model seems to be copied from a French Dinky Toy, while the box style is clearly inspired by Norev.
Price guide: £100

SPAIN

Comando Volkswagen Barcelona Taxi

The black and yellow livery of Barcelona's taxis dates back to 1934 and has inspired many different models. Although Volkswagen Beetles have been used as taxis in some countries (such as Mexico), Comando may simply have repainted its 6 inch-long Beetle model in these colours as a way of creating another variation.
Price guide: £75

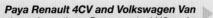

Paya Seat 1400C Barcelona Taxi

The distinctive sharp-angled lines of this car were designed by Pininfarina, who was also responsible for the Austin A55 Cambridge and other BMC cars of the early sixties. The Paya model is in 1/32 scale and, like most toys of this kind, is friction-powered.
Price guide: £50

Paya Renault 4CV and Volkswagen Van

Unlike most of the other Spanish models shown here, these Payas are to 1/43 scale. The 4CV is closely based on the French Norev model (pictured on page 30), while the VW seems to be copied from a Tekno diecast from Denmark.
Price guide: £75 each

Rico Seat 1400C Policia
Described as being to 1/38 scale, the Seat comes as a saloon, police car, taxi, estate car and ambulance.
Price guide: £75

Rico DKW F1000L Minibus
Although a German prototype, the DKW van was built under licence in Spain. Versions of the Rico include a television van, ambulance, fire van, and this school bus. Rico also made a much larger version.
Price guide: £80

Rico Pegaso Z-103 Sports
The Pegaso was a Spanish performance car, built in very limited numbers. This rare Rico model is in 1/36 scale.
Price guide: £95

Rico Pegaso Frigorifico Van
Rico made several trucks with this stylish Pegaso cab, the refrigerated van being the most desirable.
Price guide: £90

Rico Pegaso Gas Cylinder Truck
The gas canisters carried on this truck are moulded in rows rather than separately.
Price guide: £75

Rico Seat 1500 Ambulance
Another version of the Seat, this time in a larger (9 inch) size. This model also comes in fire livery, and as a green 'Policia' saloon and black/yellow Barcelona taxi.
Price guide: £60

Guisval Berliet GAK truck with barrel load ▶

Guisval is still a well-known name in Spanish diecast, but in its early days the company made some plastic models, of which this 1/43 French Berliet truck is probably the most desirable. It comes with various different bodies.
Price guide: £25

PA Seat 600 ◀

PA stands for Plasticos Albacete, which made this 5.5 inch Seat 600 in the 1970s in a style very similar to earlier Paya and Rico models. The plastic is painted rather than pre-coloured.
Price guide: £25

PA Renault R5 Policia ▶

Another model from the same series. Others in the range included a Renault R16, Citroën 8, Citroën Dyane and Seat 124.
Price guide: £15

PA Ford Fiesta ◀

As Ford built the Fiesta in a plant at Almusafes, near Valencia, it proved a popular subject for Spanish toy makers. This realistic version is 7 inches long.
Price guide: £10

PA Ford Fiesta set ▶

The Fiesta was supplied to shops in trade boxes of ten. There are four different metallic colours – gold, green, maroon and silver – and some of the cars have paper stickers such as 'Auto Escala' (driving school) or the logo of the Spanish airline 'Iberia'.
Price guide (boxed set): £100

PA Renault 12 Bomberos ▶

This Renault fire car is to a slightly larger scale (length: 8 inches) but, like the others, it has a friction motor.
Price guide: £15

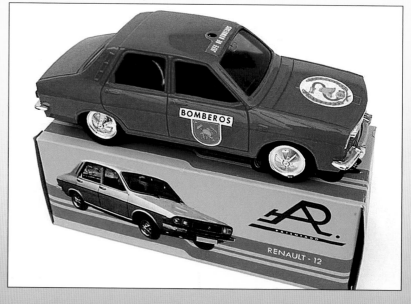

Karpan Ford Fiesta S
Founded in 1965, Karpan is still in existence today, making plastic toys such as tricycles and ride-on trucks for infants. This large (10.5 inch) Fiesta Mark One has an interior made not of plastic or tin but of printed cardboard.
Price guide: £25

Caramello Pegaso Van
Another version of the popular Pegaso van. This was really a novelty item which came in various liveries, each with a packet of sweets in the rear compartment. Scale is approximately 1/43.
Price guide: £10

VAM Land Rover
A simple toy moulded in soft plastic, this Land Rover is to approximately 1/43 scale. VAM was based in Zaragoza.
Price guide: £5

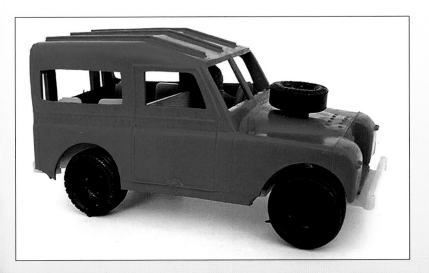

Anguplas
Anguplas made a vast series of 1/86 models in the early 1960s, and its history has been traced in depth in a book by Spanish enthusiast Juan Mauri Cruz (see bibliography). Pictured here are (left to right, clockwise): Seat 1400 van, Ford Anglia, Jaguar Mk. IX, Seat Serra Sports.
Price guide: £20 each

Ingap

Ingap is one of the oldest and most significant names in the Italian toy industry. The name is an acronym for 'Industria Nazionale Giocattoli Automatica Padova', which was founded in Padua shortly after the First World War to manufacture tinplate cars, aeroplanes, trains and other mechanical novelty items.

As happened in other countries, Ingap started to move over to plastic in the 1950s and produced cars in scales ranging from 1/24 to 1/75. The smaller cars, made between approximately 1958 and 1965, were sold in boxed sets as they were too small and cheaply made to be worth marketing individually. The trucks are crude and non-prototypical, but the cars are rather more interesting.

At least two sets are known: the first contains twelve cars, a Rolls Royce Silver Cloud, two Citroëns (a DS19 and Traction Avant), an MGA hardtop, Jaguar XK120, Mercedes 300SL, Volkswagen Beetle, Nash Metropolitan, Chrysler Imperial, Fiat 1100, Alfa Romeo Giulietta Sprint and a Lancia Aurelia. With three British, two German, two French and three Italian subjects, the set has a very cosmopolitan flavour.

Construction could hardly be simpler: a plastic body, plastic base and grey plastic wheels. Unusually, the Ingaps are moulded in a pale green plastic and then painted, rather than following the usual practice of being moulded in different colours. Realism varies: the MGA is barely recognisable but the Jaguar and Volkswagen are quite acceptable likenesses. The Chrysler is appealing as it is the only one in a two-tone colour scheme.

Some years later, the boxed set of twelve was followed up by a set of eighteen, twelve of them American cars: Fords (Galaxie, Falcon, Country Squire and Thunderbird); Chevrolets (Impala, Station Wagon, Corvair and El Camino); Cadillac Fleetwood and Eldorado, a Chrysler and a Dodge Dart. These are accompanied by six European cars: a Simca Aronde, Opel Rekord, Lancia Flavia, Fiat 1500, Ford Anglia and Austin A40.

In 1/43 scale, Ingap offered a set containing an Alfa Romeo Giulia TI, Ford Taunus 17M, Fiat 1300, Rolls Royce Silver Cloud, Citroën DS and Mercedes 220SE, plus a selection of racing cars.

It is only to be expected that an Italian company would concentrate on cars made at home, and Ingap made as many as thirty

The Alfa Romeos by Sam Toys are much harder to find than the smaller trucks.

1/32 scale Fiats, ranging from vintage cars of 1919 onwards up to the 600 and 1800 saloons of the sixties. Among these Fiats, it is something of a surprise to find an Austin A40 – though this is a perfectly logical choice as that car was sold in Italy under the Innocenti name. The large (c.6 inch) size of these models allows for refinements such as a tinplate base and bumpers, separate headlamp lenses, a friction motor, rubber tyres (marked 'Ingap – Padova') and, most interesting of all, a colourful lithographed tinplate interior. It's almost as if Ingap was reluctant to abandon altogether the original raw material in which it had developed considerable expertise over so many years. Other interesting models in this series, in addition to the many Fiats, include a Ford Anglia, Volkswagen Beetle and Renault Dauphine. Later issues are rather more cheaply finished, with plain tinplate interior pressings and a black plastic base.

Sam Toys and ICIS

Ingap's factory was in the town of Padua; further west, in Milan, three other toy companies ventured into the plastic car market in the late fifties and early sixties.

Two of these made little impact. Sam Toys made a relatively small range which divides neatly into three categories: 1/43 racing cars, 1/50 trucks and military vehicles and, by far the most interesting, a group of Alfa Romeos which look a little smaller than 1/43. Although most of its products are original designs, Sam Toys did not mind borrowing from other sources: some of the trucks are based on the Dinky Toys Military Ambulance while the pictures of the Alfas in the catalogue appear to be based on models by an Italian diecast company, Mercury. In 1965, the moulds for the Sam Toys racing cars and Alfa Romeos found their way to Eastern Germany where they were reissued under the name of Espewe, remaining in production until circa 1972.

An even more obscure Italian range than Sam Toys is a group of a dozen or so 1/43 plastic cars issued under the ICIS name around 1959-60. Consisting entirely of Italian cars – Fiats, Lancia, Alfas and a Ferrari – these are not well-known but fetch very high prices on the rare occasions when they surface on the collectors' market. ICIS cars are made of a glossy plastic and are fitted with window glazing and plated parts.

Politoys

The ICIS range was short-lived but Politoys proved that there was a market for this kind of toy car in Italy. Founded in 1955 by Eugenio Agrati and Ennio Sala, Politoys is believed to have made a small number of toy cars and trucks in approximately 1/35-1/40 scale, but little is known about these. Considerably more successful was the

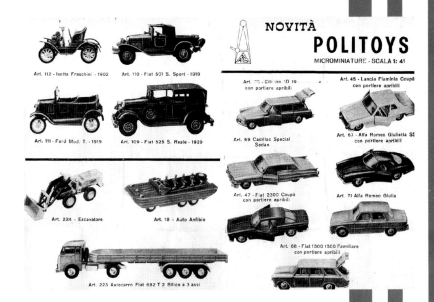

Plastic cars in 1/41 scale by Politoys.

Micro Miniatures series of plastic military vehicles in a smaller c.1/50 scale, many of them drawing inspiration from contemporary Dinky, Corgi and other ranges. Between 1960 and 1965 this range grew rapidly to include more than 150 subjects, mostly Italian and other European cars in the unusual scale of 1/41. Politoys cars have a rather heavy look to them, making them less realistic than the likes of Norev, but they are not unattractive. As well as modelling most of the Fiats and Alfa Romeos of the period, Politoys made a number of veteran cars and some impressive articulated trucks and tankers which, being in 1/41 scale, were fairly large items.

The success of the plastic series gave Politoys the confidence to compete with the big players in diecast metal, with a range of high-quality models in 1965. Cost-cutting reduced quality in the seventies, though, and Politoys moved further from its origins by adopting the name Polistil instead, to avoid confusion with the better-known Palitoy brand.

Meanwhile, the earlier plastic models found a new lease of life as the moulds were reused by a company called McGregor which, in spite of its Scottish-sounding name, was based in – of all places – Mexico.

www.velocebooks.com/www.veloce.co.uk
All current books • New book news • Special offers • Gift vouchers

ITALY

◀ **Ingap Truck**
A simple plastic truck dating from the 1950s, with a tin base and friction drive to the front wheels. Length: 7 inches.
Price guide: £30

Ingap Renault Dauphine ▶
Ingap made a number of 6 inch friction drive cars with attractively lithographed tinplate interiors. All had grey plastic tyres marked 'Ingap Padova'.
Price guide: £60

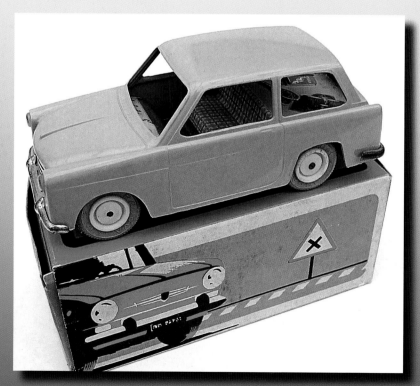

◀ **Ingap Austin A40**
In the early 1960s Innocenti, an Italian engineering company, built BMC (British Motor Corporation) cars under licence, which is why the Austin A40 was often modelled in Italy. This is another from the Ingap series of 6 inch friction cars.
Price guide: £40

Ingap Citroën DS 19 ▶

This Citroën is roughly to 1/43 scale. It was supplied as part of a boxed set with five others: Ford Taunus 17M, Mercedes Benz 220SE, Fiat 1300, Alfa Romeo Giulia TI and Rolls Royce Silver Cloud. The Citroën is the most sought-after.
Price guide: £30

◀ **Ingap Fiat 1100**
Ingap supplied some cars to a Milan mineral water company as part of a promotional offer. These are easily distinguished from regular issues, being marked 'Achille Brioschi and Co Milano' underneath. No interior fittings or friction motors were fitted.
Price guide: £40

Ingap Ford Anglia ▶
This Anglia is a later issue: the tin base has been replaced by a black plastic one, and although the interior is still tinplate, it lacks the lithographed details and is plain grey. Length: 6 inches.
Price guide: £40

Ingap set

The twelve models are: Rolls Royce Silver Cloud; Jaguar XK 120; Volkswagen; Fiat 1100; MGA; Alfa Romeo Giulietta Sprint; Lancia Aurelia sports; Mercedes 300SL; Nash Metropolitan; Citroën Traction Avant and DS; Chrysler Imperial. Each car is approximately 2.5 inches long.
Price guide: £40

Sam Toys Jaguar D Type

One of a series of 1950s racing cars, this Jaguar resembles a British diecast model by Crescent. The axles are fitted with spring suspension. Length: 4.25 inches.
Price guide: £25

Sam Toys Alfa Romeo Giulietta Spider

Sam Toys also made a few Italian cars which are much harder to find than the racing cars. At 3.5 inches long, this convertible is nearer 1/50 than 1/43 scale.
Price guide: £60

Politoys Ford Taunus 17M

Politoys cars were described as being 1/41 scale, which makes them look quite large alongside regular 1/43 size models.
Price guide: £50

Politoys Alfa Romeo Giulietta T1
One of the harder to find models in the 1/41 scale series. Most of the cars carry licence plates with the letters 'MI' for Milan.
Price guide: £60

Politoys Alfa Romeo Dauphine ▶
In 1958 Alfa Romeo made an agreement with Renault which allowed the Dauphine to be assembled and distributed in Italy, which explains why this model is described as an Alfa Romeo.
Price guide: £45

◀ **Politoys Fiat 615N**
As well as cars and large trucks, Politoys made some light commercial vehicles, such as an Alfa Romeo van and pick-up and this Fiat minibus.
Price guide: £45

Politoys Lancia Flaminia ▶
Launched in 1957 and still available in 1970, the Flaminia was a luxury car built in small numbers. The two-tone colour division on the Politoys model is achieved by moulding the body in two sections.
Price guide: £50

Politoys Volkswagen 1500
Like the famous Beetle, the 1961 VW 1500 was rear-engined. The Politoys version is not the most accurate likeness.
Price guide: £45

Politoys Autobianchi Bianchina Panoramica
The Autobianchi was based on the Fiat 500 but had a more stylish body. This Politoys version features opening rear and side doors.
Price guide: £45

Politoys Alfa Romeo 2600 Police Car
Another later Politoys issue with opening doors, in 'Squadra Mobile' colours.
Price guide: £40

Politoys Radar Truck ▶

Politoys made a large number of military vehicles. This American GMC truck was also available with a machine gun, rocket launcher or searchlight.
Price guide: £20

◀ **Dulcop Mini**

Dulcop was an obscure company, based in Bologna, which made some plastic military vehicles and a few cars, including a Fiat 127, Volkswagen, and this Mini.
Price guide: £10

CGGC Volkswagen set ▶

This Volkswagen carries a logo with the letters 'CGGC' underneath and comes on a backing card with tools and figures.
Price guide: £15

GERMANY

From the late nineteenth century onwards, Nuremberg enjoyed the reputation of being the world's centre of metal toy production. Inevitably, the First and Second World Wars dealt the industry a heavy blow and allowed other countries the opportunity to catch up.

In 1945, the Nuremberg toy industry had effectively to start from scratch. One favourable factor, however, was the city's location in the American-occupied zone, once again allowing access to the lucrative American export market. Toys were produced in exchange for the foreign currency that would provide vital basic supplies – summed up at the time in the slogan 'tinplate for tinned food'.

Thus, the toy industry shared in the German 'economic miracle' of the 1950s. However, in the long term, the writing was on the wall. The market for tin toys was completely taken over by Japan, where labour costs were much lower and where there was no reluctance to copy other companies' products. In any case, by the mid-1950s, traditional tin toys had had their day, falling out of fashion because of safety concerns over their sharp edges.

Willingly or otherwise, long-established German toy companies such as Distler, Arnold, JNF and Gama started to make use of plastics for their clockwork, friction and battery-powered cars. JNF is a typical example. The letters stand for Josef Neuhierl, in Fürth, who founded his company in 1920. JNF started making tin cars again after the Second World War, bringing out the 'Struxy' series of plastic cars in 1960. As the name suggests, these had a construction element as the car could easily be taken apart and put together again. Models like the 1/25 scale Mercedes 220S and the larger (12 inch) Volkswagen Karmann Ghia T34 are highly prized by German collectors, though the type of plastic used is prone to warping unfortunately. This series lasted for only a short time, until JNF devoted its attention to an electric slot car system before disappearing from the scene in the 1980s.

By then, of course, many other famous German toy names had disappeared, too. A major factor in this decline was that many companies continued production of metal toys for too long, failing to recognise the importance of plastic.

One exception to the rule was Gama, founded by Georg Adam Mangold, in Fürth, in 1882. After the Second World War, Gama produced many tinplate cars, its masterpiece being a 1950s Cadillac. The appearance of a plastic 1959 Buick Electra inaugurated a new series which can be seen as transitional products, combining plastic bodies with lithographed tinplate interiors. Gama then concentrated its efforts on the 'Mini-Mod' series of diecast cars, which enabled the company to survive and to take over another famous German brand, Schuco, in the 1980s.

If some of the older German metal toy companies saw plastic as a threat, there were others who embraced the new material wholeheartedly. Most mechanical tin toys were necessarily large and therefore expensive; plastic, on the other hand, was well adapted to smaller and cheaper lines. Germany's biggest contribution to the development of plastic cars was to lie in small HO scale models, originally envisaged as accessories for model railways.

The key figure here was Friedrich Karl Peltzer. Being the son of a naval officer, Peltzer was always interested in ships and his hobby was making waterline models of these. In 1938, he made a scale model vehicle and exhibited at a trade fair in Leipzig, founding Wiking Modellbau the following year. He hardly had time to develop the business when war broke out, and during this period, Peltzer's

The Gama factory in Fürth, Germany, as it looked in 1965.

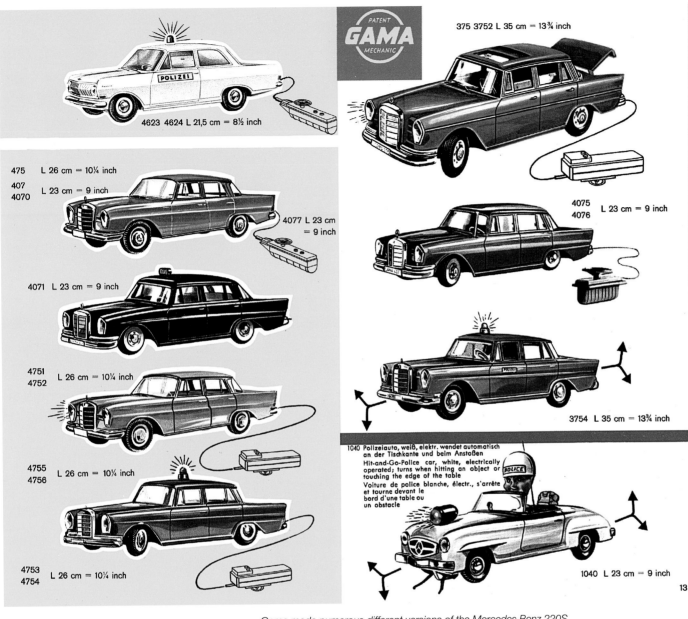

abnehmbar
Taxi-Mercedes 220 S, steerable, patent clockwork, Taxi-plate detachable
Taxi Mercedes 220 S, mécanique à ressort brevetée, plaque »taxi« mobile, roues orientables
4751 Mercedes elektr. mit Fernsteuerung (3 V.)
Mercedes, electric-motor (3 V.) with remote control
Mercedes téléguidée électrique (3 V.)
4752 Mercedes wie No. 4751, blinkende Richtungsanzeiger
Mercedes as No. 4751, blinking direction indicators
Mercedes, même modèle que 4.751 mais clignotants de directions
4755 Mercedes Polizei-Auto, grün, elektr., Blaulicht, Friktion
Mercedes police-car, green, electr. blue-light, friction
Mercedes de police à friction, verte, lumière bleue
4756 Wie No. 4755, weiß
as No. 4755, white colour
Modèle 4.755 mais couleur blanche
4753 Polizeiauto, wie No. 4755, Elektromotor m. Fernlenkung, Sirene
Police-car, as No. 4755, electric motor with remote control, siren
Voiture de police, modèle 4.755 mais téléguidée électr. avec sirène
4754 Wie No. 4753, weiß
as No. 4753, white colour
Modèle 4.753 mais couleur blanche
375 Mercedes 220 S, Schiebedach, Kofferraum z. Öffnen, Friktion
Mercedes 220 S, sliding roof, trunk compartment can be opened, friction
Mercedes 220 S à friction, toit et coffre ouvrants
3752 Mercedes wie 375, elektr. (3 V) Fernsteuerung, blinkende Richtungsanzeiger, Schiebefenster
Mercedes as No. 375, electric (3 V) remote control, blinking direction indicators, sliding windows
Modèle 375 mais téléguidé électr. (3 V.), clignotants de direction et fenêtres ouvrantes
4076 Mercedes 220 S, Elektromotor (1,5 V) vor- und rückwärts, Radio-Antennenschaltung
Mercedes 220 S, electric (1,5 V) forward and back, radio antenna gearing
Mercedes 220 S électr. (1,5 V.) marches avant et arrière, mise en marche par antenne radio
4075 Mercedes wie 4076, Fernlenkung
Mercedes as No. 4076, remote control
Modèle 4.076 mais téléguidé électrique
3754 Mercedes Polizeiauto, wie 375, elektr. (3 V) Wendewerk, Blaulicht, Sirene
Mercedes Police car as No. 375, electric motor (3 V), automatical turning device, blue light, siren
Mercedes de police comme No. 375, téléguidée électrique (3 V.), lumière bleue et sirène. Changement automat. de direction
13

Gama made numerous different versions of the Mercedes Benz 220S.

company made training models for the German military. After the war, he had great success making plastic toy vehicles, particularly 1/40 scale promotional models for Volkswagen, original examples of which are highly prized today. Das 'Gläserne' Auto was a Volkswagen Beetle, with a transparent plastic body and separate chassis components that came in assembly kit form. Thereafter, other versions of Volkswagen vehicles – the Beetle, the Transporter Van, Karmann Ghia coupé and VW 1500 – were to follow. Most Wiking models, however, are in HO scale. Reflecting the flavour of the period in which it was made, the first issue was an American military Jeep, followed by an American sedan in 1949. Early issues had solid one-piece bodies without the windows being cut out. Window glazing first appeared in 1957 and interior fittings in 1966.

Of course, the Wiking company did not have the market to itself. Another significant range of plastic cars was made by Siku, a trademark registered in 1950 by combining the first two letters of 'Sieper', the family who owned the firm, and 'Kunststoff', German for plastic. The history of the Sieper company, however, goes back much further to 1921, when Richard Sieper started making metal cutlery in Lüdenscheid. Later product lines included military belts, buttons and decorations, and even the three-pointed star bonnet emblem fitted to Mercedes cars. Some clockwork and friction drive plastic vehicles were made in the early 1950s, as well as plastic figures and animals. 1955 marked a turning

A page from Wiking's 1964 catalogue of HO scale plastic cars.

point for the company as a range of plastic cars was launched, their slightly larger scale of 1/60th differentiating them from the 1/87 Wikings. At first, these were exclusively based on German Volkswagen, Opel, Borgward, Mercedes, Ford and DKW cars, with various American, French and Italian subjects being added later. Some of these were supplied in an ingeniously designed perspex case which could double as a lock-up garage, though the more elaborate commercial vehicles came in conventional cardboard boxes. Siku models carried a catalogue number prefaced by a 'V', starting with V1 (a Mercedes 300 saloon) and reaching over 200 by the time that plastic gave way to diecast metal in 1963, though some of the plastic models lasted for a few more years.

Another toy company that made plastic cars in the town of Lüdenscheid was Artur Hammer. Its first efforts were similar in size to Wiking, but later a group of 1/80th scale cars was introduced. These were made in two sections with the roof being moulded separately, usually in white. This construction method gave the cars their characteristic two-tone style. The series consisted of eight German cars: a Mercedes 220 and 190SL, BMW 507, Opel Kapitan and Caravan (estate car), Volkswagen Karmann Ghia, DKW 1000 and a Borgward Isabella Coupé. There were also numerous trucks and buses in a similar scale. In the early 1970s, a group of six 1/50th cars followed – Mercedes 250, Fiat 1800, Ford Taunus 20M, Volkswagen 1600TL, Audi 100 and BMW 2000.

Hammer's most interesting products are a group of realistic 1/50th scale sports cars with separate windscreens and interiors (Triumph TR4, Auto Union, MGA, Porsche cabriolet, Fiat 1500 and Alfa Romeo Giulietta Spider) and a three inch-long Volkswagen van/bus, again moulded in two halves. As this was frequently used as a promotional item, many different variations can be found.

Hammer ceased producing toy cars in the seventies, but Wiking and Siku are still very much part of the current model car scene. In fact, these two famous names have now joined forces. The death of Wiking founder, Friedrich Peltzer, in 1981, led the company to be taken over by Siku in 1983, though the brand identities of both ranges have been maintained. Thus, Siku is still a well-known name in diecast while Wiking continues to be the leader in the field of HO plastic models. With the growing interest in collecting plastic models, Wiking started reissuing earlier 1/40th scale Volkswagen promotional models in 1994.

Arnold Renault Floride

The firm of Karl Arnold was founded in Nuremberg in 1906 and was well-known for tin toys. In the early 1960s, some cars were made with tin bases and plastic bodies, such as this stylish Renault Floride, available in both friction and cable-operated form. Length: 9.75 inches.
Price guide: £60

Gama Opel Rekord ▶

A very detailed replica of the 1959 Opel Rekord, featuring plated bumpers and grille, headlamp lenses, whitewall tyres and a lithographed tin interior – complete with camera and magazines on the rear parcel shelf! Length: 8.5 inches.
Price guide: £75

Gama Mercedes Benz 220S Taxi

Always a popular choice with German toymakers, the Mercedes was modelled by Gama in two sizes, this version being the smaller one. Length: 9 inches.
Price guide: £75

Gama Opel Kapitan ▶

Like the Rekord and Mercedes, this Opel Kapitan is friction-powered.
Length: 9 inches.
Price guide: £75

GERMANY

JNF Struxy Mercedes 220S
Like Arnold and Gama, JNF turned from tin to plastic in an attempt to survive in the competitive market of the 1960s. The Mercedes is friction driven and measures 7.75 inches in length.
Price guide: £90
(Courtesy www.gasolinealleyantiques.com)

JNF Struxy Volkswagen 1500
At 8.5 inches in length, this VW is to a larger scale than the Mercedes (nearer 1/20 than 1/25). Unfortunately, the plastic used on Struxy cars tends to warp.
Price guide: £90
(Courtesy www.gasolinealleyantiques.com)

Siku DKW van
The Siku 'V' series of 1/60 scale models was launched in 1955. The boxes were designed in the style of a garage.
Price guide: £25

Siku Ford Taunus
To avoid its cars having too lightweight a feel, Siku fitted a metal weight inside.
Price guide: £25

Siku Opel Rekord ▶

The two-tone effect is achieved by moulding the body in separate sections.
Price guide: £25

◀ **Siku Opel Rekord**
A later model of the Rekord dating from 1961. Cars in the 1/60 series were typically around 3 inches in length.
Price guide: £25

Siku Edsel ▶

Being much larger than European cars, the Edsel stretched to 3.75 inches and required a larger garage to accommodate it.
Price guide: £25

◀ **Siku VW Kombi**
No German toymaker could overlook the VW van and Siku modelled it as a minibus, pick-up and delivery van.
Price guide: £30

Siku Citroën DS ▶

Unlike the other models, in this case the two-tone effect is achieved by painting the roof.
Price guide: £25

◀ **Wiking 1/40 scale Volkswagen**

An extremely rare example of a promotional model produced in the early 1950s for Volkswagen. Described as 'Das Gläserne Auto', the transparent plastic bodyshell allows the interior and driver to be seen. This 4.25 inch long model features the split rear window fitted to pre-1953 Beetles.
Price guide: £450
(Courtesy Alex J. Cameron)

Wiking VW 1500

The Wiking Volkswagens were clipped together and could therefore be dismantled. As such, Wiking took considerable trouble to make the interior as detailed as the exterior.
Price guide: £60

Wiking Trambus Senator
To cater for export markets the box of this HO scale model carries German text on one side and English on the other, where the bus is described as a 'Viking model made by experts with care and efficiency'.
Price guide: £20

Wiking Berliner Doppeldeck Bus
Double decker buses are mostly British, but this one is based on a prototype used in Berlin. The advertising is represented by waterslide decals.
Price guide: £20

Novy Simca 1000
A 1/43 French Simca is an unusual choice of car to be made in Germany. Marked in French underneath 'Modèle Salon (Paris) 1961', it may have been made as a promotional item. This appears to be the only model by Novy.
Price guide: £25

Hammer Bus
This M.A.N. coach has the upper half moulded in transparent plastic. Hammer made several buses using the same method of construction. Length: 4.25 inches
Price guide: £9

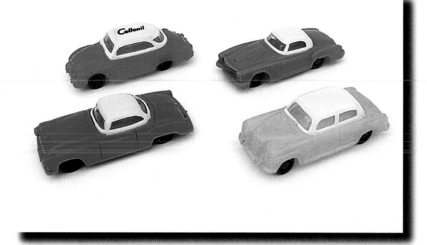

Hammer Cars
Again, these cars are made in two parts, with the white roof separate from the body in each case. Back row: DKW and Mercedes 190SL; front row: Borgward Isabella and Mercedes 220.
Price guide: £5 each

Hammer Sports ▶
Hammer's convertibles were slightly larger than the other cars. The yellow one is an MGA while the green car looks like an American Ford Thunderbird but is, in fact, a DKW 1000SP. Length: 3 inches.
Price guide: £10 each

Hammer VW Van
The three-inch VW van appeared in many promotional liveries. This one, 'Schuh-Neumann', advertises shoes.
Price guide: £15

Hammer VW Van ▶
This 'Nivea' van has window glazing and may therefore be a later issue.
Price guide: £10

Tempo Pick-Up ▶

Although there is no clue to the maker, this Tempo pick-up is marked 'Frankonia Vollmilch Schokolade' and may have been given away as part of a promotion. *Length: 3.5 inches. Price guide: £15*

◀ **Repair Truck**

Marked 'W. Germany', this simple repair truck is another typical toy made of softer plastic. *Length: 3.5 inches. Price guide: £5*

Citroën DS 19 ▶

A four inch Citroën, again marked 'W. Germany' underneath. *Price guide: £10*

◀ **Saloon Car**

A fragile late 1940s style of saloon car with friction motor, marked 'Made in Germany'. *Length: 5 inches. Price guide: £15 (Courtesy Douglas R. Kelly)*

Opel Rekord
An ingeniously designed Opel Rekord with removable roof sections allowing an estate car, saloon or convertible to be created. Length: 5 inches.
Price guide: £25
(Courtesy Douglas R. Kelly)

Auto-Dux electric 800 set
A scarce set which allows five different Volkswagen models to be constructed: Beetle, 1500 saloon, Microbus, van and pick-up, each model being 4-5 inches in length. The vehicle can then be operated via a remote-control.
Price guide: £200
(Courtesy Alex J. Cameron)

Dux Volkswagen Beetle and VW 1500
Two cars from the set: VW 1500 (left) and Beetle (right). The angle of the front wheels can be altered by moving a lever under the bumper.
Price guide: £35 each
(Courtesy Alex J. Cameron)

USA

The United States was the most prolific source of plastic toys in the post-war period, and the history of the companies who made them has been well-documented in a number of books. Essentially, American plastic toys fall into three distinct categories. The earliest were designed as inexpensive playthings, cheap enough for a child to buy with his pocket-money. In the United States, they're nicknamed 'dimestore dreams' and one American collector, Bill Hanlon, used that term as the title for a book on the subject.

The first injection-moulded plastic toy car is believed to have been made by Kilgore of Ohio in 1938, quickly followed by similar vehicles by Lapin Products Inc. However, it was really in the late 1940s that demand grew and Hanlon has painstakingly chronicled the toy cars of companies like Ideal, Renwal and Processed Plastics. Rather like Norev in France, Renwal takes its name from the surname of its founder, Irving Lawner, spelt backwards. Renwal started by making plastic furniture for dolls' houses, branching into toy vehicles around 1947. The Ideal Novelty and Toy Company had prospered during the Second World War by making plastic parts for gas masks, and introduced a toy Jeep in 1944. One interesting aspect of American plastic toy production is that the chemical corporations which made the raw materials, such as Monsanto Chemical Co and the Celanese Corporation, were very active in promoting the manufacture, sales and distribution of plastic toys, placing press advertisements and compiling catalogues for toy wholesale buyers.

It was not only between the chemical and toy industries that a partnership existed; plastic cars proved of considerable interest to the motor industry, too. In 1948, demand for new cars far outstripped supply, giving a man called West Gallogly the idea of making a cast aluminium (or 'aluminum' as it is spelt in the USA) model of a Ford to display in showrooms, allowing prospective customers to see the range of colours available on the real car. Such models came to be known as 'promotionals' and although Gallogly named his company AMT ('Aluminum Model Toys'), he soon discovered that plastic was a more economical material to use. AMT's first plastic promotional was a 1949 Ford, moulded in an acetate material known as Tenite, and before long, all the major American automobile corporations were

1952 trade advertisement for Monsanto's 'Lustrex' plastics pointed out the advantages of plastics for toys.

The most wanted toys this Christmas are made of LUSTREX *Styrene Plastic*

New plastic toys are more ingenious, more realistic— better than ever before

By Marion Palmer, Modern Living Consultant

Plastic toys are *newer, safer, sturdier* this year!
NEW—with the educational, true-to-life realism that children love.
SAFE—with smooth, easy-to-clean surfaces and bright, "clear-through" colors that can't chip or peel or rust.
STURDY—there are sturdy and durable plastic toys today, many of them made of Monsanto's new, *tougher* Lustrex styrene plastic that's especially good for toys.
And you'll find most plastic toys are more economical, too. Be sure your youngsters have the *most wanted* toys this Christmas—toys made of plastics.
MONSANTO CHEMICAL COMPANY, Plastics Division, Springfield 2, Mass.

MONSANTO

SERVING INDUSTRY . . . WHICH SERVES MANKIND

It's Edsel Showtime on the Road

ROAD-CHECK THE BIG ONE —
GET A LITTLE ONE <u>FREE</u>

$2 precision scale model Edsel yours as a gift when you take the test drive of a lifetime!

(Offer limited to adults only)

In the medium-priced field
**THE ONE THAT'S REALLY NEW
IS THE LOWEST PRICED, TOO!**

Postcard sent out to prospective buyers to entice them to test-drive the Edsel in exchange for a free plastic promotional model.

commissioning models of their cars, either from AMT or from another similar company, Jo-Han. Car salesmen quickly realised that, as one slogan of the time put it, 'the little ones sell the big ones', and the promise of a free toy car for the kids would lure many a family into the showroom to book a test drive.

Plastic toy cars could be used to promote other products than real motor vehicles, such as breakfast cereals. The F&F Mold and Die Works of Dayton, Ohio, made plastic novelty lines – one of them being a five inch salt and pepper set in the shape of two negro figures, 'Aunt Jemima and Uncle Mose'! F&F found a lucrative niche in supplying small (3 inch-long) plastic cars as part of on-pack cereal offers. Ford and Mercury models predominate, although other makes of car were represented too, as well as trucks and buses.

By the mid-1950s, a third category of plastic toys was emerging: the construction kit. The earliest of these was Revell's 'Highway Pioneer' series, followed in 1955/56 by some American cars in 1/32 scale. Revell and AMT pooled their resources and from 1958 onwards, many of the larger promotional models were also issued in unassembled form. For its part, Ideal issued the 'Cars of all Nations' series, which included some unusual subjects like the Spanish Pegaso. This range was available in the UK by arrangement with O and M Kleeman Ltd who used the 'Kleeware' name, while Revell (GB) started making kits in 1957. In that year, it was estimated that 62 per cent of American families with children had one or more members who occupied themselves by assembling plastic kits. Plastic construction kits are, of course, a specialised hobby of their own and are outside the scope of this book.

As had happened in other countries, American toy companies already established in other fields started to make use of plastic too. The most significant of these is Hubley, whose history stretches back as far as 1893. In that year, John Edward Hubley, a bank employee in Lancaster, Pennsylvania, developed a business out of his hobby of making cast iron toys and founded the Hubley Manufacturing Company. Hubley introduced die-cast toys in the 1930s, and in 1950 built a new plastics moulding factory in Lampeter, Pennsylvania. The previous year, a six inch car model, based on a Packard, had been introduced, and can be found in numerous colourful taxi and fire chief liveries. This model was announced in the 1949 catalogue as being available in a boxed set of three taxis or as part of an 'Auto Set' containing a sedan, taxi and two fire engines. Numerous plastic trucks, tractors and roadbuilding equipment followed in the early 1950s. In 1962, Hubley entered the plastic kit market with a series of eight 1/24 scale cars. The first was an American Ford Country Sedan, but the others were based on European cars. Hubley was taken over by Gabriel Industries in 1966.

Another famous name in the American toy industry was Marx, founded in 1919 by Louis Marx, the son of a German immigrant. So successful was this brand, that it is said that at one time about one-fifth of all toy production in the USA carried the Marx logo. The development of the company follows a pattern which is very similar to many others examined in this book: success with tinplate mechanical toys in the pre-war years was followed by a move into plastic in the 1950s. The first Marx plastic model, a replica of a Yellow Cab, actually appeared in 1948. Marx later made a range of cars in around 1/43 scale with simple plastic bodyshells and heavier metal wheels, such as a Chevrolet Corvair, Ford Fordor and Studebaker Champion. Some of these were supplied in toy garage sets.

As the next chapter demonstrates, plastic production in Hong Kong eclipsed other countries in the 1960s. Seeing the direction in which the tide was flowing, Marx moved production there and, under the name 'Elm Toys', manufactured a series of very attractive HO scale plastic models. The series comprised some forty different vehicles, some of them not unlike the German Wiking models in appearance. There was also a tie-in with the Disney company, leading to some of the Elm Toys being fitted with drivers like Mickey Mouse, Donald Duck and other cartoon figures!

Eventually, indigenous Hong Kong plastic toy makers were to take over the production of Marx toys altogether. However, the moulds of many of the originals survived and these were reissued for the collectors' market in the 1990s – including the very first plastic Marx car, the Yellow Cab.

www.velocebooks.com/www.veloce.co.uk
All current books • New book news • Special offers • Gift vouchers

AMT 1949 Ford ▶

This is one of the very earliest plastic toy cars to have a battery-operated remote-control. The 1/25 scale Ford was AMT's first car to be made from a plastic acetate material called 'Tenite', with sheet metal 'glazing' for the windows in order to conceal the mechanism inside. The model was available in three versions: freewheeling, clockwork and electrically-powered. According to the box of the maroon coloured car, it was powered by 'a five pole electric motor encased in methyl methacrylate' which was 'moisture proof and dustproof'.
The grey car is an earlier version of the Ford which has the rear door handles in the wrong place. As it is unlikely that AMT would have made such an obvious error, it may be that the model was based on a pre-production sample of the real Ford and that this door arrangement had been considered at the design stage.
This example is clockwork-powered, with a non-removable key fitted underneath the tinplate base, which accounts for the rather high ground clearance of the model.
Price guide: £100 each
(Courtesy Alex J. Cameron)

▲
Hubley Packard Taxi
This 6 inch Packard was first shown in Hubley's 1949 catalogue. It also came as a Fire Chief's car.
Price guide: £20
(Courtesy Alex J. Cameron)

◀ **Renwal Garage Set**
From 1947 onwards Renwal was a major name in American plastic toys. This garage set with two vehicles was made between 1953 and 1955. Each truck is just over 3 inches long.
Price guide: £50

Renwal Taxi
This 6.5 inch taxi dates from 1949-1951. Unusually for the period, the doors and boot lid open and there is a spare tyre in the boot.
Price guide: £40
(Courtesy Douglas R. Kelly).

Renwal Cement Mixer
Another late 1940s/early 1950s Renwal product. Pushing the truck along moves a worm gear which rotates the mixer. The silver handle behind the door and the wheel and deflector at the rear are usually missing on surviving examples.
Price guide: £50
(Courtesy Douglas R. Kelly)

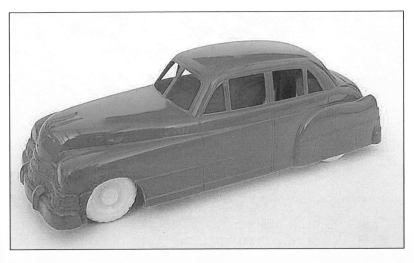

Lapin Cadillac
Lapin Products Inc. of Newark, New Jersey, first made plastic moulded cars just before the Second World War. This 6 inch Cadillac dates from the early 1950s.
Price guide: £10

Lionel Ford ▶
Lionel was a famous American make of model railways rather than cars, but this 1955 Ford Customline was produced to go on a car carrier wagon. Various colours were available. Length: 5 inches.
Price guide: £10

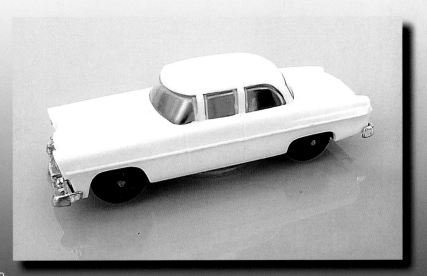

Irwin Studebaker

A larger and more sophisticated plastic toy which represents the legendary 1953 Studebaker coupé designed by Raymond Loewy. The model has a friction motor and an interior of printed cardboard. Length: 9.5 inches.
Price guide: £60

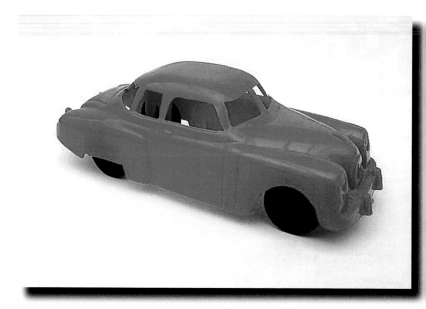

Marx Studebaker ▶

A model of the famous Raymond Loewy-designed 1950 Studebaker Champion by Marx. Length: 3.75 inches.
Price guide: £15

◀ Marx Cadillac

Another simple Marx plastic car, based on a 1960 Cadillac 62. Length: 4.5 inches.
Price guide: £8

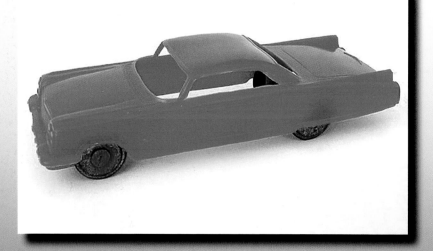

Processed Plastics Cadillac ▶

Processed Plastics of Aurora, Illinois, made this four inch 1955 Cadillac Eldorado convertible with the hood in a different colour.
Price guide: £8

Processed Plastics Jaguar XK150 ▶

A larger car from the same firm, this Jaguar has added refinements such as a driver, folded hood, steering wheel and windscreen. Length: 7.5 inches.
Price guide: £15

◀ **Gilmark Jaguar**

The Gilmark Merchandise Corporation of New York made some 4 inch 'Build-a-Car' models which could be quickly snapped together. This is a Jaguar XK 120.
Price guide: £12

Plasticville Garage ▶

As the name suggests, Plasticville was a series of plastic buildings made as accessories for model railways. Simple plastic vehicles were available to accompany these.
Price guide: £25

◀ **F & F Ford set**

F & F made three inch plastic cars which were given away with breakfast cereals. This selection of five Fords dates from 1955.
Price guide: £40 (boxed set)

Wyandotte Milk Truck
The origins of Wyandotte can be traced back to 1921 when the company was originally known as All Metal Products. This 5 inch plastic milk van is friction-powered and dates from 1952.
Price guide: £50

ARCO Triumph ▶
A 4 inch polythene Triumph TR sports car. The number plate carries the letters 'ARCO' which stand for Auburn Rubber Co.
Price guide: £7

Soft plastic Mercedes and Talbot
Two other soft American plastic cars based on European subjects: the Mercedes 300SL and an unusual French Talbot. Both are 4.5 inches long.
Price guide: £7

HONG KONG

revious chapters have demonstrated how the variety of plastic toys available in European countries increased rapidly during the 1950s. However, developments on the other side of the world were to have a dramatic effect on the European toy industry.

After the Communist takeover of China in 1949, the British colony of Hong Kong witnessed an influx of Chinese refugees and this availability of cheap labour proved to be a major factor in the colony's rapid economic growth over the next decade. Hong Kong quickly became one of the world's major producers of toys and fancy goods, churning out vast quantities of plastic items very cheaply. That, of course, was bad news for British toy companies who complained loudly about unfair competition.

Worse still, many Hong Kong toys were only too obviously copied from British products. As the copies were made without permission, most Hong Kong toymakers tended not to draw attention to themselves by putting their names on their toys, simply marking them as 'Empire Made' or 'Made in Hong Kong' – an expression that soon came to be thought of as synonymous with 'cheap quality'. If the toy does not have its original box, it can be difficult to identify who made it.

Even if the box is still present, many mysteries remain, as more often than not, the packaging carries the name of the distributor rather than the maker. For example, Telsalda, the best known Hong Kong plastic toy brand, was not a toy manufacturer but a London-based importer that had been bringing in textiles from the Far East since 1890. The picture painted by the British toy industry of unscrupulous Hong Kong toymakers imitating its products and selling them back to the United Kingdom was misleading. The practice was, in fact, for UK toy buyers to go out to Hong Kong with samples of British toys and negotiate with plastic manufacturers via an agent, giving an order to the factory that would copy the toy at the cheapest price.

These plastic copies were usually scaled up versions of Dinky and Corgi cars, the larger dimensions allowing for the fitting of a friction motor inside. Such toys are often found in boxes carrying names such as 'Clifford Series', 'Fairylite', 'OK', 'Emu Series' and 'Laurie Toys', all of which were trademarks of distributors. Similarly, 'Cragstan' was a New York-based toy importer. Sometimes, buyers from large stores would place orders for plastic toys, such as those sold exclusively in branches of F. W. Woolworth under the 'Woolbro' name. In time, as the Hong

Kong industry became more experienced in its business practice, toy manufacturers such as Lucky Toys began to market their own products.

The best-known indigenous Hong Kong plastic toy brand is probably Blue Box. This company, founded in 1952 by Peter Chan Pui, originally became successful by making toy dolls. Blue Box then moved into toy cars, happily borrowing ideas from diverse European manufacturers. Many small Matchbox cars were copied and issued in various garage sets, but other toys clearly take their inspiration from Dinky, Corgi and Wiking products.

All of this had profound consequences for the American and European toy industries. In the face of Hong Kong competition, it was no longer economic to manufacture large-scale plastic friction or battery-operated cars such as those made in Germany by Gama or in Britain by Tri-ang Minic. Tri-ang, and others, turned instead to the development of slot car systems that were more fun to play with.

On the principle that if you can't beat them you may as well join them, well-established names began to source manufacture of their own toys in Hong Kong. The American toy giant Louis Marx, for instance, had set up a factory in Britain in 1932 and had built a new one in Swansea, Wales, in 1948 but saw the direction in which things were moving and opened a new factory in Hong Kong in 1956. The British factory remained open until the mid-1960s, but by that time Marx's Hong Kong workforce was 1000-strong. Production of toys made in the UK factory was transferred to the Far East – one of the first examples of a trend that is familiar in British industry to this day.

Today, most toys of whatever kind are sourced from the Far East, and although many toy corporations have head offices in Hong Kong, manufacturing facilities are now situated in China. Companies like Blue Box are now much more sophisticated operations, making pre-school toys and collector figures based on fantasy characters in video games. According to its website, 'Blue-Box has evolved into a world class, totally integrated manufacturing, sales and marketing organisation'.

The toys pictured here represent only a small selection of the vast number of plastic vehicles made during the 1960s. Most take their inspiration from contemporary diecast models and while they were originally viewed with disdain as inferior imitations, these plastic look-alikes are now every bit as sought-after as the diecast metal originals on which they are based.

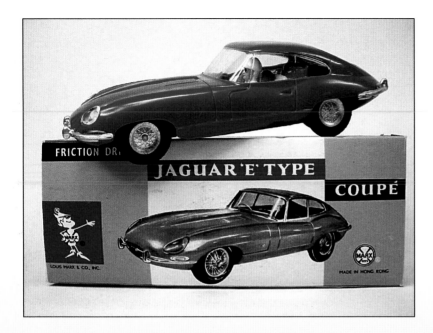

Marx Jaguar E-type
This 8 inch long friction E Type comes with a driver wearing goggles and helmet. In the rear compartment are his luggage and golf clubs.
Price guide: £70
(Courtesy www.gasolinealleyantiques.com)

Ford Mustang ▶
Marked with a logo of a globe, but no maker's name, the Mustang can also be found in red with an ivory interior. The boot opens to reveal three pieces of luggage.
Length: 8.25 inches.
Price guide: £70
(Courtesy www.gasolinealleyantiques.com)

◀ **LB Ford Thunderbird**
This 7 inch toy represents the third generation Ford Thunderbird launched in 1961. The car is powered via a hand-held battery box.
Price guide: £35

Cadillac Convertible ▶

An impressive 10 inch model which resembles the 1963 Cadillac from the front. It is fitted with a driver, steering wheel and separately glazed lights front and rear. There is a logo underneath but no indication of the maker's name.
Price guide: £50

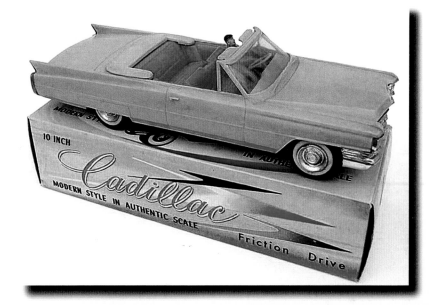

◀ **Standard Vanguard**

Most Hong Kong copies were to a larger scale, but this Vanguard is roughly the same size as the Corgi Toy on which it is based.
Price guide: £15

Austin Cambridge ▶

Another from the same series, also based on a Corgi Toy. Although neither cars nor boxes carry identification marks, they have been seen in trade packs marked 'Irene Series'.
Price guide: £15

Lincoln Jaguar Fire Chief Car ▶

This battery-operated Jaguar features 'automatic action': when the car approaches an object it reverses and turns away. It even has a flashing roof light. Length: 9 inches.
Price guide: £60

◀ **OK Jaguar XK120**

This Jaguar is clearly marked with the 'OK' brand name, distributed in the UK by Don Bricks Ltd, 530-4 Kingsland Road, London E8. According to the box, this toy is 'a medium to develop children's intelligence'. Length: 5.5 inches.
Price guide: £40

CM Austin Cambridge ▶

The Austin A60 Cambridge was in production between 1961 and 1969. This plastic replica has similarities with the Corgi diecast. Length: 6 inches.
Price guide: £35

Lucky Toy Vauxhall Cresta
Not all Hong Kong toys were copies – no diecast model of this Cresta was made. Like contemporary diecasts, it features an opening bonnet and engine.
Price guide: £25

Mak's Mercedes Benz Racing Car
Mercedes Benz returned to motor racing in 1954 with the W196. In real life the car was silver. This 6 inch version has four separate side exhaust pipes and a driver. The artwork on Mak's boxes was always to a high standard.
Price guide: £30

OK Mercedes Benz 220SE
A friction drive Mercedes featuring separate plated door handles and a three-pointed star bonnet mascot. OK also made a slightly larger version of the same car, with an electric motor.
Length: 7.5 inches.
Price guide: £30

SK Ghia
Only 26 examples of this exotic vehicle were built between 1960-62, one of them being owned by Frank Sinatra. This 5 inch plastic version is probably based on the Corgi diecast. It is battery-operated.
Price guide: £15

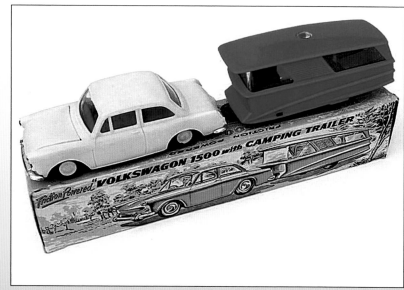

HP Volkswagen 1500
The 6 inch Volkswagen is a scaled-up version of the Dinky Toy original, while the caravan is based on an Italian Politoys model. The VW also comes separately as a fire chief's car.
Price guide: £60

OK Rolls-Royce
A good quality model, with many separate fragile components such as handles on the doors and boot lid, silver lady mascot – and even separate indicator lenses.
Length: 7 inches.
Price guide: £35

Lucky Toys Rolls-Royce with Horsebox

Both these items are clearly marked with the horseshoe logo of Lucky Toys. The 5 inch Rolls Royce is based on a Dinky model while the horsebox can be found attached to other vehicles, too.
Price guide: £30

Lucky Toys Duesenberg and Ford

Two 5 inch long cars from the Lucky Toys 'Old Timer series', both of them based on 1930s prototypes.
Price guide: £5 each

Jimson E-type

This little model is difficult to find because it is so fragile. It was probably not sold separately but may have come as part of a car transporter set.
Price guide: £10

Blue-Box Jaguar Mark Ten ▶

Blue-Box models were often crudely made but attractively presented. In this set, the car is based on a Corgi Toy while the figures were part of the Dinky range.

Price guide: £30

◀ **Blue-Box Bedford Farm Truck**

An interesting hybrid which appears to combine a copy of the Dinky Bedford TK cab with the rear section of the Corgi Dodge Kew Fargo livestock truck.

Price guide: £15

Blue-Box Maxwell Roadster ▶

Blue-Box freely borrowed from many different sources. This is a close copy of the Matchbox Yesteryear – even the colour scheme is the same.

Price guide: £8

Blue-Box MG Sports
This is clearly a copy of a Dinky Toy. The box style, too, is very similar except that it is, of course, blue rather than yellow.
Price guide: £15

Blue-Box Volkswagen Rally Car ▶
A slightly later Blue-Box product, dating from the early 1970s. The 'rally' element consists of nothing more than a sticker on each side door reading 'Monte Carlo 77835', the number simply being the catalogue reference number of the toy.
Price guide: £20

Blue-Box Express Coach
This is a slightly scaled-up version of the German Wiking model of a Bussing Trambus which is pictured on page 75. Length: 6 inches.
Price guide: £10

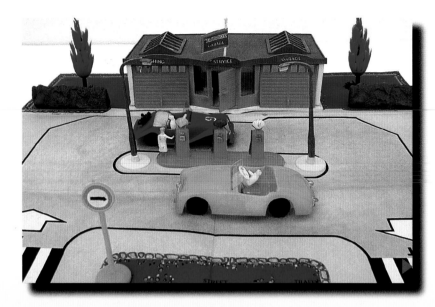

Blue-Box Garage Set

A delightful set which captures the simple charm of Blue-Box plastic toys. It contains an MG, Austin Healey, a garage, and numerous accessories.
Price guide: £35

OK Albion Tipper ▶

Unusually for a 1960s Hong Kong plastic product, the box of this toy carries patent numbers for the UK, USA and West Germany. Length: 5 inches.
Price guide: £25

OK Albion Pipe Transporter

An original subject, with considerable play value, this transporter matches the Albion cab unit to a trailer carrying twelve plastic pipes that can be joined together.
Length: 13 inches.
Price guide: £50

Cragstan Austin Articulated Lorry ▶

The inspiration for this probably comes from the Tri-ang Spot-on series which joins tractor to trailer with a similar spring-loaded coupling. Length: 8.5 inches.
Price guide: £30

◀ **Telsalda Ambulance**

This model is closely based on the Spot-on Wadham's ambulance. The rear doors open to reveal a stretcher and two attendants. Length: 6 inches.
Price guide: £40

Jimson Farm Truck ▶

A more original design than most Hong Kong products, this farm truck comes complete with four plastic pigs! Length: 8 inches.
Price guide: £30

ACME Petrol Tanker ▶

A scaled-up version of a Corgi model of an ERF truck. Acme eliminated the central pillar of the windscreen, oerhaps to give the truck a more modern appearance.
Length: 7.5 inches.
Price guide: £30

◀ CM London Routemaster Bus

London buses were very popular subjects for Hong Kong-made toys, as they were often sold in souvenir shops in the capital. Length: 6 inches.
Price guide: £15

NFIC Leyland Atlantean Bus ▶

This 5 inch bus is similar in size to the Dinky Toy on which it is based. The box illustration shows the red and white livery used on the Dinky original.
Price guide: £10

BOAC Coach
Another bus closely modelled on a Dinky Toy. The example shown is friction-powered, but a remote-controlled battery-operated version also exists.
Price guide: £25

Touring Bus ▶
Probably produced some years earlier than many of the other models pictured here, this touring bus is made of a hard, brittle plastic and resembles a Mercedes prototype. It carries no identifying marks. Length: 6 inches
Price guide: £25

Mak's Fire Engine
The Commer fire engine was one of the most popular and long-running Dinky Toys, and it is not suprising that it was copied in Hong Kong. The friciton motor imitates the sound of a siren. Length:6 inches.
Price guide: £30

Mak's International Step Van
Most Hong Kong plastic toys are based on British vehicles but the step van was an American concept. This also comes as a mail van. Length: 4.5 inches
Price guide: £25

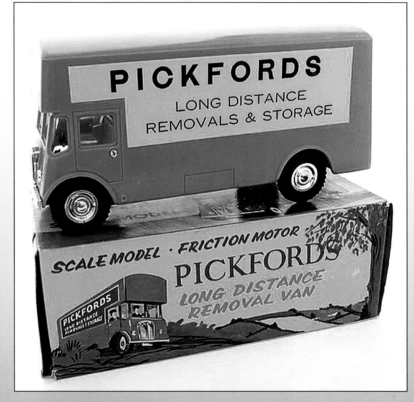

Fairylite Pickford's Van ▶
Matchbox made a Pickford's furniture van but this one is much bigger (7 inches long). The van comes in light blue or red, whereas in real life Pickford's used a dark blue livery.
Price guide: £40

Clifford Series VW Camper
This, too, recalls a model in the Matchbox range. The side doors open and, like the real VW van, the motor – in this case a friction mechanism – is at the rear.
Length: 6 inches.
Price guide: £35

Telsalda Road Roller ▶

The inspiration for this 5 inch model comes from a French Dinky Toy, the Richier road roller which first appeared in 1958.
Price guide: £25

▲ Telsalda Ford Thames Minibus

This model comes with a removable roof rack, luggage and passengers. Another variation has an extended roof section as fitted to the original Corgi camper van from which it is copied. Length: 7.5 inches.
Price guide: £35

Linda Toys Tipper ▶

This simple truck is 4.5 inches long. Linda Toys also made copies of some early Corgi Toy cars, such as a Rover, Jaguar and Citroën.
Price guide: £8

Matchbox copies ▶

Many different copies of the popular small Matchbox series were made in Hong Kong. Shown here are a Leyland Coach, Austin Taxi and Rolls Royce Silver Cloud.
Price guide: £6 each

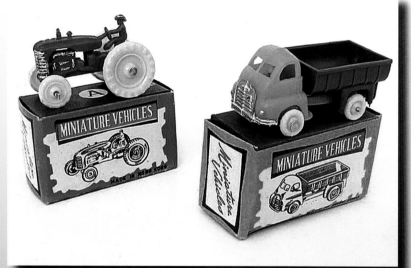

◀ **Matchbox copies**

Two more Matchbox lookalikes, the Massey Harris Tractor and Bedford tipper, both made of a softer plastic material.
Price guide: £5 each

www.velocebooks.com/www.veloce.co.uk
All current books • New book news • Special offers • Gift vouchers

OTHER COUNTRIES

This book has attempted to show a representative sample of the toys made by most of the major plastic manufacturers in Europe and the USA. There are, of course, hundreds of other plastic toy cars that have been made all over the world. This final chapter presents a small selection of the vast number of items originating from countries as far apart as Greece, Argentina, Czechoslovakia and Portugal, with one even coming from as unlikely a place as Guadeloupe!

Diverse as these toys are, a common theme is that many are either copied from the products of mainstream manufacturers or are made from the same tooling.

Roco of Austria, for instance, made a set of four plastic cars in around 1960 which are clearly based on German Siku models: a Ford Taunus estate car, a DKW, an Opel Kapitan and an American Edsel. Each came in four different colours, making a total of sixteen variations to collect. Roco made another set of four to a larger c. 1/43 scale, this time resembling contemporary diecast models – a BMW 507 and a Mercedes 300SL based on German Marklins, and a Jaguar 2.4 and Bentley Continental that look very like British Corgi Toys. Apart from these eight cars, Roco is best known for its own line of plastic military vehicles.

The same combination of duplication and innovation has been repeated many times elsewhere. In Portugal, for example, some plastic copies of early Wiking Volkswagens were in circulation under the name Ribeirinho. Like some of the French plastic manufacturers based in Oyonnax, this company was founded in 1905 to make horn combs. After the Second World War, José Teixeira, the son of the founder, started making toys in plastic and his copies of the 1/40 Wiking Volkswagen were still being produced in the 1970s. A similar Portuguese company was Osul, founded in the 1940s by Artur and Alfonso Henriques. Wiking influence was also apparent in its early products but it went on to make many interesting plastic cars, such as an Isetta bubble car, a Citroën DS19 and the two Ford Taunus estate cars pictured in this chapter. Osul is best known for the 'Metosul' diecast series.

In Greece, some larger-scale plastic clockwork-powered cars were made by Elvip. Both the Ford Taunus model and its box are similar to a German Gama model, suggesting that the Greek version may have been made from the same mould once Gama was finished with it. Another Greek brand, Joy Toy, made some buses which have similarities with German plastic models as well as issuing various sports and racing cars – notably an MGA – and Bedford Trucks which seem to be its own designs. Most Joy Toy models are crisply moulded in quality plastic, and some of them carry the year '1970' on the number plate which helps to date them. The Joy Toy range was made by the Vitalis Brothers, which is 'Adelphoi Bital' in Greek, hence the 'AB' logo to be found underneath the models.

Unlike these minor toy manufacturers, Lego of Denmark is world famous and this company, too, turned its expertise in plastics towards the production of toy cars. Founded in 1932 by Ole Kirk Christiansen, Lego's early products were in fact made of wood. From about 1950, however, Lego made an extensive range of plastic trucks in approximately 1/40 scale, though they were all variations on just two basic models, a Chevrolet lorry and delivery van. These were later joined by an extremely rare 1/35 scale Volkswagen Beetle. More familiar is Lego's range of HO scale cars, Bedford and Mercedes trucks, which have a slightly heavier and more substantial feel than other similar toys because of their shiny metal wheels. The cars were cleverly packaged in transparent plastic garages designed to fit together with Lego building bricks.

It is common practice in the toy industry for redundant moulds to be sold to countries where the industry is less developed, with the result that an obsolete toy can often find a second lease of life elsewhere. This is how Italian Politoys tooling came to be issued in Mexico under the McGregor name. Similarly, some ex-Minialuxe moulds found their way to Argentina and thereafter to Colombia, where plastic cars were issued under the Simex name. Other South American products, like those of Hong Kong, are not direct copies or reissues of European products but are clearly based on the same designs. A case in point is the fire engine by Chibi of Argentina, which is a scaled-up plastic replica of the popular Dinky Toy Turntable Fire Escape. The crudely-made 1/15 scale Citroën 2CV marked 'Produccion LS' is copied from an earlier Japanese tin toy by Daiya – right down to the style of artwork on the box. On the other hand,

South American toy companies were quite capable of coming up with well-made products of their own design. The high quality 1/25 scale DKW made in Brazil by ATMA Paulista of Brazil is just one example. Undoubtedly, many other unusual items from this part of the world have yet to be discovered by European collectors.

The same is true of the plastic cars made in Eastern Europe and Russia. Both the quality and the originality of some of these are remarkable. In East Germany, a number of 1/20 scale battery-powered cars based on subjects such as the Tatra and Wartburg were made by Presu, while at the opposite end of the spectrum in terms of size, Espewe made a large range of HO scale plastic vans, trucks and cars. In 1965, Anker brought out a 1/30 scale Wartburg 311 saloon and kombi (estate car), and in the 1970s made a whole series of 1/25 scale replicas of the Barkas delivery van and minibus, as well as a Trabant 601. Russian cars were also frequently modelled in plastic, from the humble Zaz (Zaporozhets) to the Chaika limousine. Even in the 1970s and 1980s, Russian plastic toys were still being made in a style that recalls European products of twenty years earlier, giving them an instant appeal to collectors.

In addition to these indigenous products, the redundant tooling of many European toy companies found its way across the iron curtain over the years, and plastic reissues of French Norevs, Italian Politoys and Mebetoys often surface on the collecting market. Many of the toy cars made in the Soviet Union were therefore based on typically French vehicles like 1960s Simcas and Panhards, which would never have been seen on the roads of Moscow!

In Czechoslovakia, Igra produced a series of 1/43 scale plastic vintage cars and also made numerous models of Skodas and Tatras. KDN acquired some moulds from Politoys of Italy and was still turning out cars like the Citroën DS19, Ford Anglia and Austin A40 in the 1980s.

The number of plastic cars made outside the major European toy-producing countries is truly vast and there is no doubt that many more discoveries remain to be made. These pages can do little more than hint at the hidden potential of this collecting field.

A leaflet illustrating some of the HO scale cars in the Lego range.

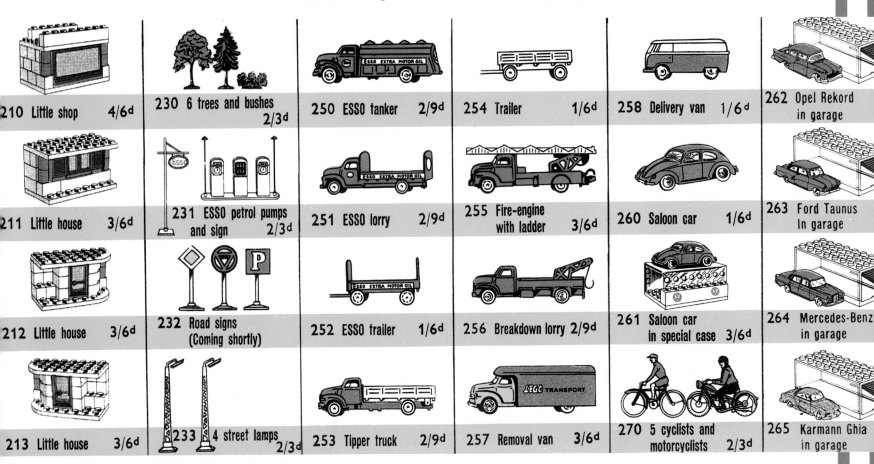

210 Little shop   4/6d

230 6 trees and bushes   2/3d

250 ESSO tanker   2/9d

254 Trailer   1/6d

258 Delivery van   1/6d

262 Opel Rekord in garage

211 Little house   3/6d

231 ESSO petrol pumps and sign   2/3d

251 ESSO lorry   2/9d

255 Fire-engine with ladder   3/6d

260 Saloon car   1/6d

263 Ford Taunus in garage

212 Little house   3/6d

232 Road signs (Coming shortly)

252 ESSO trailer   1/6d

256 Breakdown lorry 2/9d

261 Saloon car in special case   3/6d

264 Mercedes-Benz in garage

213 Little house   3/6d

233 4 street lamps 2/3d

253 Tipper truck   2/9d

257 Removal van   3/6d

270 5 cyclists and motorcyclists   2/3d

265 Karmann Ghia in garage

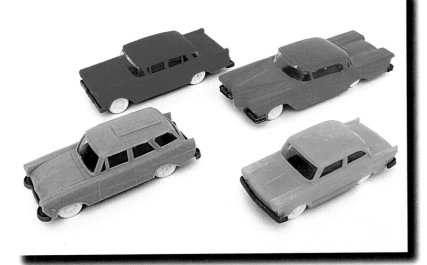

Roco set
Made in Austria, this set comprises four 1/60 cars that are similar to those made in Germany under the Siku name.
Price guide: £20

Roco Bentley ▶
Roco made another set of four in approximately 1/43 scale. This Bentley Continental resembles a Corgi Toy.
Price guide: £10

◀ **Roco BMW**
Another from the 1/43 set, a BMW 507 similar to the one modelled by the German Märklin firm.
Price guide: £10

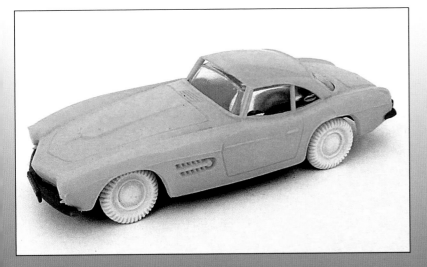

Ribeirinho Volkswagen ▶
A copy of the German Wiking promotional, made in Portugal. Although it represents the early 'split-window' Beetle, this copy dates from the 1970s.
Price guide: £10

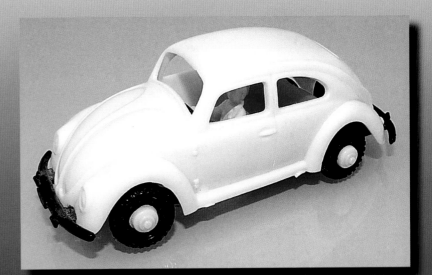

OTHER COUNTRIES

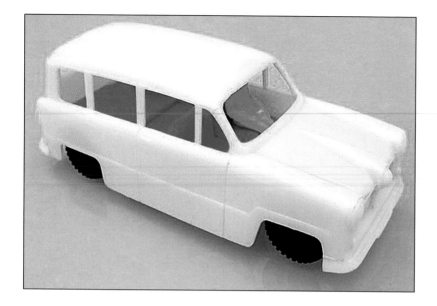

Osul Ford Taunus Estate Car

A very unusual early product by Osul of Portugal. Made of hard plastic, this 4.75 inch Ford Taunus estate car has an opening rear door and a fold-down seat.
Price guide: £25

Osul Ford Taunus 17M ▶

A later Taunus, the 1960-64 17M, also from Osul, but slightly bigger at 5.5 inches and made of a softer plastic. Unusually, only the windscreen is glazed.
Price guide: £25

Radar Mercedes Benz 300SL

The famous Mercedes Gullwing was popular with many toy manufacturers. This 1/43 scale version is by Radar of Portugal.
Price guide: £10

Pepe Mercedes Benz Taxi ▶

Although it is very much in the 1960s style, this Portuguese taxi was, in fact, produced in the 1980s. It has a friction motor and also comes as a yellow Madeira taxi.
Price guide: £10

Luxor Pick-up ▶

A product of Luxor Plastics, Amsterdam, Holland, this 4.5 inch pick-up is fairly unremarkable in itself and is of interest chiefly for its box which is designed in the shape of a garage. It looks as if it dates from the early 1950s.
Price guide: £30

◀ **Lego**

As well as plastic bricks, Lego produced some high quality HO scale cars and trucks, such as this Volkswagen 1500.
Price guide: £20
(Courtesy Douglas R. Kelly)

Lego ▶

Another from the Lego series, this Morris 1100 was designed to appeal to the British market.
Price guide: £20
(Courtesy Douglas R. Kelly)

OTHER COUNTRIES

Lego ▶
A more elaborate Mercedes articulated truck by Lego.
Price guide: £30
(Courtesy Douglas R. Kelly)

◀ Wittrock Tourist Bus
H Wittrock was active as a maker of plastic toys in Copenhagen, Denmark between 1948 and 1955. This tourist bus is very similar to a German Wiking model. Boxed examples of Wittrock toys are extremely rare.
Price guide: £80

Lemezarugyar Citroën DS 19 ▶
Made in Budapest, Hungary, this series included a Volkswagen, Mercedes Benz 220, Fiat 600 and this Citroën. All are made of a strong, heavy plastic material.
Length: 6.25 inches.
Price guide: £15

Lemezarugyar Volkswagen
Another of the same series. The base is of tinplate and incorporates a friction motor.
Price guide: £15

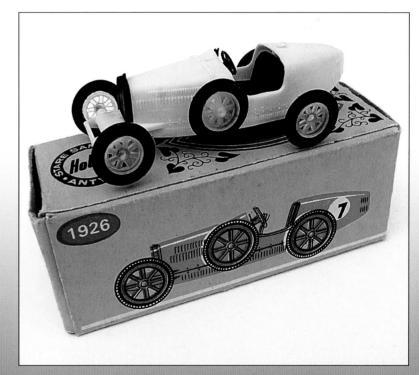

Estetyka Bugatti ▶
This delicate 3 inch model of a Bugatti 35 was made in Poland. It appears to be based on the Matchbox Model of Yesteryear.
Price guide: £4

◀ **Smer Skoda**
Smer was a Czech company which began making plastic cars such as Skodas and Tatras in the 1950s, using a hard bakelite type of material. Length: 3 inches.
Price guide: £10

OTHER COUNTRIES

Presu Tatra T603

The original V8 rear-engined Tatra dates from 1934 but the model shown here represents the T603 which came out in 1956 and remained in production for some eight years. This 11 inch plastic model was made by Presu of East Germany, whose range also included a Wartburg and a Chevrolet convertible.

The box is marked 'Ferngelenktes Elektro-Spielzeugauto' which simply means 'remote-controlled electric toy car'. The unusual frontal arrangement of the real car, with three headlamps behind a glass lens where the radiator grille would normally be, is faithfully reproduced – and the headlamps light up, too.
Price guide: £100
(Courtesy Alex J. Cameron).

KDN Fiat 1100

Also from Czechoslovakia is KDN, short for Kovodružstvo Náchod. KDN issued a series of plastic cars using ex-Politoys moulds from the 1960s.
Price guide: £5

KDN Ford Anglia

Another from the same series. These toys were still easily obtainable in the 1980s.
Price guide: £5

KDN Austin A40 ▶

Apart from the KDN logo underneath, there is little to distinguish these models from the original Politoys.
Price guide: £5

▲
Piko Barkas Minibus

This 1/25 scale model was originally made by Anker of East Germany in the early 1970s. From 1974 the brand name was changed to Piko. Length: 7.25 inches.
Price guide: £10

ARI Unic Tipper ▶

ARI stands for August Riedeler of Königsee, a long-established East German manufacturer of dolls. Some time in the 1960s the company came to an arrangement with the French Norev firm to produce some Norev Unic trucks, such as this tipper.
Price guide: £25

OTHER COUNTRIES

Joy Toy MGA and Bedford TK

The MG is 3.5 inches long and the Bedford tipper 4 inches. The latter carries the date '1970' on the number plate. Although both are British vehicles, the models come from Greece.
Price guide: £5 each

Joy Toy Bedford Artic

Another variation on the Bedford cab unit. This 'Sea-Land' box van is 8.75 inches long.
Price guide: £7

Elvip Ford Taunus Station Wagon

Elvip stands for Elliniki Viomichania Paichnidion, which means 'Greek toy industry'. Both the box and the car itself are similar to a model in the German Gama range, though the plastic used is of poorer quality. The Ford is clockwork-powered and is 8 inches long.
Price guide: £35

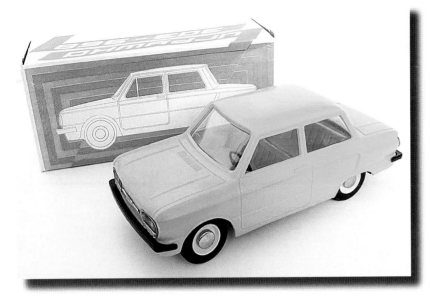

Zaz
Zaz is short for Zaporozhets, a rear-engined Russian car dating from 1967 with styling similar to the German NSU Prinz. This high quality plastic model is battery-operated and has electric lights.
Price guide: £35

Zaz ▶
A smaller and much more cheaply made version of the previous car.
Length: 4 inches.
Price guide: £6

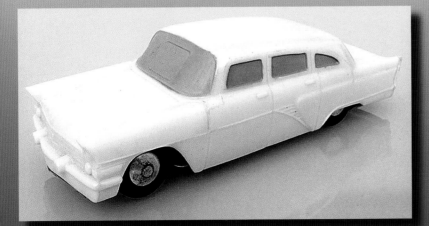

Chaika
The Chaika was a Russian limousine with styling influenced by the American Packard of 1955. The car was in production until 1976, though only about 2,000 were built. This friction toy is made of a thick Bakelite type of material.
Price guide: £20

OTHER COUNTRIES

Limousine
Another Russian toy, made of a much lighter plastic. Length: 4 inches.
Price guide: £10

Russian Mercedes Benz 250 Coupé ▶
Many obsolete Western toy cars were later reissued in Russia. This Mercedes was originally made by Mebetoys of Italy.
Price guide: £12

RyM Peugeot 504
The fact that Peugeots were assembled in Argentina explains why models of a French car were made in that country. This one is to 1/33 scale and is marked RyM underneath.
Price guide: £20

Chibi Fire Engine ▶

A 12 inch plastic copy of the Dinky Supertoy Turntable Fire Escape, made in Argentina. There are no markings underneath, but the door stickers and box carry the name Chibi.
Price guide: £40

◀ **LS Citroën 2CV**

A Japanese tin toy by Daiya inspired this 1/15 scale plastic model which carries the logo 'Produccion LS'. It is made of a very thick plastic, the window openings are roughly trimmed by hand.
Price guide: £50

Simex Peugeot 403 ▶

This is a South American reissue from the moulds of the French Minialuxe model illustrated on page 36.
Price guide: £30

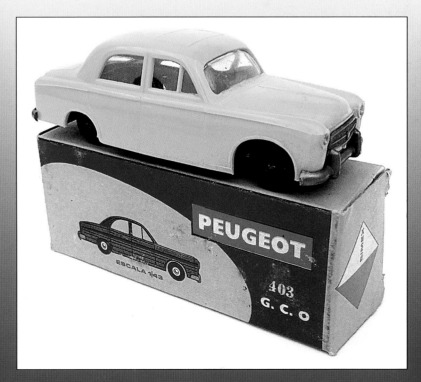

OTHER COUNTRIES

Simex Simca Oceane ▶
Another from the same series. The box is over-labelled 'Made in Argentina' but this has been scored out and 'Colombia' written instead.
Price guide: £30

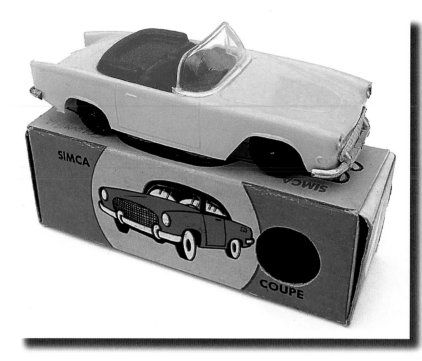

◀ DKW
Made in Brazil by ATMA Paulista, this 1/24 scale DKW is friction-driven. It is a high quality item, possibly issued as a dealer promotional model. Length: 7.5 inches.
Price guide: £100+
(Courtesy www.gasolinealleyantiques.com)

Japanese Toyota and Datsun ▶
As a generalisation, it would be true to say that Japan specialised in tin toy cars and Hong Kong in plastic. However, these three cars show that, as in other countries, Japan made transitional models combining tinplate interiors and fittings with a plastic bodyshell. The convertible is a Datsun Fairlady and the saloon a 1966 Toyota Corona.
Price guide: £25 each

Ford Fordor
The mould for this American Ford was far-travelled. Originally issued by Tudor Rose of England, this version comes in packaging marked 'Made in Mexico', with the address of a distributor in Guadeloupe! Length: 4.25 inches.
Price guide: £10

APPENDIX I:

MANUFACTURERS OF PLASTIC MODEL CARS

Company	Country	Comments
ACME	USA	Plastic vehicles
Anguplas	Spain	HO scale cars
Anker	East Germany	Friction and clockwork vehicles (1/30 and above)
ARI	East Germany	HO scale trucks, some based on French Norevs
AMT	USA	1/25 promotional cars
Banner	USA	1950s plastic toys
Beeju	GB	Simple plastic vehicles (late 1940s onwards)
Blue-Box	Hong Kong	Various scales; some with friction motors
Blue Bow	Hong Kong	Matchbox copies, similar to Blue-Box
Brimtoy	GB	Cars and trucks in various scales, combining plastic and tin
BS	France	1/43 and 1/32 cars
CM	Hong Kong	Friction cars
Cadum Pax packets	France	Mostly HO scale cars, given away in washing powder
Caramello	Spain	Pegaso Trucks
Cayro	Spain	1/43 Citroën Traction Avant
Chibi	Argentina	Friction vehicles
Chiqui Cars	Spain	A range of 1/43 cars made by Nacoral
Clé	France	1/64, 1/48 and 1/32 cars
Cofalu	France	Motorcycles and Tour de France models
Comando	Spain	c.1/32 scale friction cars
Convert	France	Promotional vans
Cragstan	USA/Hong Kong	American distributor of Hong Kong friction cars
Crio	France	Soft plastic sports/racing cars
Cursor	Germany	c.1/40 scale models
Dulcop	Italy	1/43 scale cars
Dux	Germany	Clockwork-powered cars
ECF	France	Similar models to BS
Eko	Spain	Reissues of Anguplas
Elm Toys	Hong Kong	HO scale plastic cars
Elmont	GB	Brand name for a series of plastic trucks made by Timpo

Elvip	Greece	Clockwork plastic cars
Espewe	East Germany	Trucks, military vehicles and veteran cars
Estetyka	Poland	Vintage cars
F&F	USA	3 inch promotional models
FJ (France Jouets)	France	Large scale electric cars
Fairylite	GB/Hong Kong	British distributor of Hong Kong friction vehicles
Gama	Germany	Large scale electric and friction cars
GéGé	France	1/43 and 1/20 cars
Geyper	Spain	Mercedes 220, based on a German Schuco model
Grisoni	Italy	Simple c.1/50 cars
Guisval	Spain	Vintage cars and Berliet trucks
Hammer	Germany	Range of small cars and trucks
Hercules	Portugal	c.1/43 plastic vehicles
Hubley	USA	Packard sedan and trucks
ICIS	Italy	1/43 Italian cars
Ideal	USA/Hong Kong	Plastic vehicles in various scales
Igra	Czechoslovakia	Vintage cars and East European vehicles
Ingap	Italy	Cars in various scales
Injectaplastic	France	1/43 cars and 1/33 Citroëns
ISAT	Italy	1/43 racing cars
Jean	Germany	Cars and vans in a similar style to Hammer
Jimson	Hong Kong	Friction vehicles
Johan	USA	1/25 scale promotionals and kits
Jouef	France	HO scale cars; later made slot cars
Joy Toy	Greece	c.1/43-1/50 vehicles
Jyesa (JYE)	Spain	Larger friction vehicles
KDN	Czechoslovakia	Reissues of Italian Politoys
Kilgore	USA	Pioneered plastic cars before the Second World War
Kleeware	USA/GB	Vehicles and other toys
Lapin	USA	Early post-war American plastic cars
Laurie Toys	Hong Kong	Friction vehicles
Lemezarugyar	Hungary	Friction cars
Lego	Denmark	HO cars; larger trucks and VW
Les Routiers	France	1/43 Renault Etoile Filante
Lido	USA	1950s plastic cars
Linda Toys	Hong Kong	Friction cars
Lindberg	USA	1/60 scale cars
Lionel	USA	1955 Ford Sedan
Lucky Toys	Hong Kong	Friction cars
Luxor	Holland	c.1/40 cars and trucks
LYS	Portugal	Bedford
Mak's	Hong Kong	Friction vehicles
Marquis Toys	Australia	1939 Hudson
Marx	USA/GB/Hong Kong	Large friction cars; HO scale cars

McGregor	Mexico	Reissues of Italian Politoys
Mettoy	GB	Friction vehicles in various scales
Minialuxe	France	Large range of 1/43 and 1/32 models
Minic	GB	Cars in various scales
Minix	GB	HO scale cars
Mont Blanc	France	Various cars and trucks, some with Tinplate components
Moplas	Italy	Fiat tanker
NFIC	Hong Kong	Numerous vehicles, some with friction
National Toys	Italy	Cars and racing cars
Norev	France	Large range of 1/43 and 1/86 vehicles
Nosco	USA	Clockwork vehicles, reissued in Mexico
Novy	Germany	Makers of a 1/43 Simca 1000
OK	Hong Kong	Friction vehicles
Osul	Portugal	Copies of German Wiking models; Some large scale cars
PA [Plasticos Albacete]	Spain	Friction cars
Palitoy	GB	Pioneered plastic cars after the Second World War
Paya	Spain	Mostly 1/32 and larger-scale cars
Penguin	GB	Early post-war rubber-band powered cars
Piko	East Germany	Trademark of Anker post-1974
Pilot	Denmark	HO scale cars
Plastica	France	Simple c.1/40 cars
Plasticart	East Germany	1/30 cars
Plasticville	USA	Plastic cars and buildings
Pocher	Italy	HO scale Fiats
Politoys	Italy	Large range of 1/41 scale vehicles
Poplar Playthings	GB	Polythene toy vehicles
Presu	East Germany	Large scale battery-operated cars
Processed Plastic	USA	Cars in various scales
Radar	Portugal	c.1/45 cars
Renwal	USA	Many 1950s plastic vehicles
Riberinho	Portugal	Volkswagen and VW Kombi
Rico	Spain	Many vehicles in 1/32 scale and larger
Rivarossi	Italy	HO cars and trucks
Roco	Austria	1/60 and 1/40 cars; military Vehicles
Roskopf	Germany	Military vehicles
Safir Champion	France	Plastic trucks with diecast bases
Sam Toys	Italy	1/40 and 1/50 cars; smaller trucks
Sesame	France	Plastic and tin commercial vehicles; some plastic cars
Siku	Germany	Large range of 1/60 vehicles
Simex	Argentina/Colombia	Reissues of Minialuxe
SLJ	France	Detailed c.1/20 scale friction cars
Smer	Czechoslovakia	Cars in various scales
Struxy	Germany	Large scale friction cars, made by JNF
Telsalda	Hong Kong	Friction vehicles
Thomas Toys	USA	1940s/1950s plastic toys

APPENDIX I

Tropica	France	Simple HO scale cars
Tudor Rose	GB	Vehicles, some in soft plastic
Vapé-Bourbon	France	1/43 trucks and tankers
Vercor	Spain	Friction cars
Victory	GB	1/20 electric cars
VMF	East Germany	Wartburg saloon
Wannatoy	USA	Simple plastic vehicles
Wiking	Germany	Large range in HO scale; 1/40 VW promotional models
Wittrock	Denmark	Plastic vehicles in various scales

www.velocebooks.com/www.veloce.co.uk
All current books • New book news • Special offers • Gift vouchers

APPENDIX II:
BIBLIOGRAPHY

PUBLICATIONS

Beaujardin, Didier
Le Monde Fantastique de Norev
(Editions Grancher, Paris, 2005)

Cruz, Juan Mauri
Anguplas: Historia de un sueño
(privately published, Barcelona, 2001)

Force, Edward
Classic Miniature Vehicles of Northern Europe
Covers the history of Siku.
Schiffer Publishing, Pennsylvania, 2002)

Hanlon, Bill
Plastic Toys: Dimestore Dreams of the '40s and '50s
(Schiffer Publishing, Pennsylvania, 1993)

Gärtner, Stefan and Lange, Frank
Spielzeugautos der DDR
Covers the history of East German toy companies, including many
plastic cars.
(Battenberg, Munich, 2001)

Johansen, Dorte and Hedegård, Hans
Danske Modelbiler
Covers the history of toy cars made in Denmark, including Lego and
other plastic brands.
(Samler Børsen, Copenhagen, 2002)

Kelly, Douglas R
Diecast Price Guide Post-War: 1946-Present
Contains useful background information on the history of various toy
companies.
(Antique Trader Books, Iowa, 1997)

Moro, Philippe
Hep! Taxi
Illustrates 1000 taxi models, many of them in plastic.
(Editions Drivers, Toulouse, 2005)

O'Brien, Richard
Collecting Toy Cars and Trucks
A reference book with some company histories.
(Krause Publications, Iola, Wisconsin, 1997)

Ralston, Andrew G
Toy Cars of Japan and Hong Kong
Illustrates many Hong Kong plastic cars.
(Schiffer Publishing, Pennsylvania, 2001)

Rampini, Paolo
The Golden Book of Model Cars 1900-1975
A comprehensive guide to diecast and plastic cars of the world.
(Edizioni Paolo Rampini, Milan, 1995)

Rich, Mark
Toys A to Z
A reference book with background information on many obscure
companies.
(Krause Publications, Iola, Wisconsin, 2001)

Walsdorff, Rüdiger
Wiking: die Peltzer-Ära
History of the German Wiking company.
(Portus Verlag, Berlin, 2004)

Ward, Arthur
Airfix: Celebrating 50 Years of the Greatest Plastic Kits in the World
(Harper Collins, London, 1999)

APPENDIX II

WEBSITES

www.madmalc.screaming.net/victoryindex.htm
Provides a detailed history of Victory plastic cars.
www.geocities.com/peacehaven2001/index.html
Illustrates many of the British 'Beeju' plastic toys.

www.plastikauto.de
Provides full details of numerous ranges of small scale plastic cars made in Germany, including Hammer.

www.87thscale.info
Lists a vast number of makers of HO scale cars, many of which were made in plastic.

www.wolfsburgwarehouse.com
A source of interesting Volkswagen models.

www.wiking.de
The official website of the German Wiking firm, giving a history of its development.

www.gasolinealleyantiques.com
The website of an antique toy dealer based in Seattle, USA, which lists rare plastic models for sale.

www.autominiatures.com
The website of collector Alex Cameron, illustrating many unusual plastic models.

www.diecastcollector.com and www.modelcollector.co.uk
Websites of UK toy collectors' magazines.

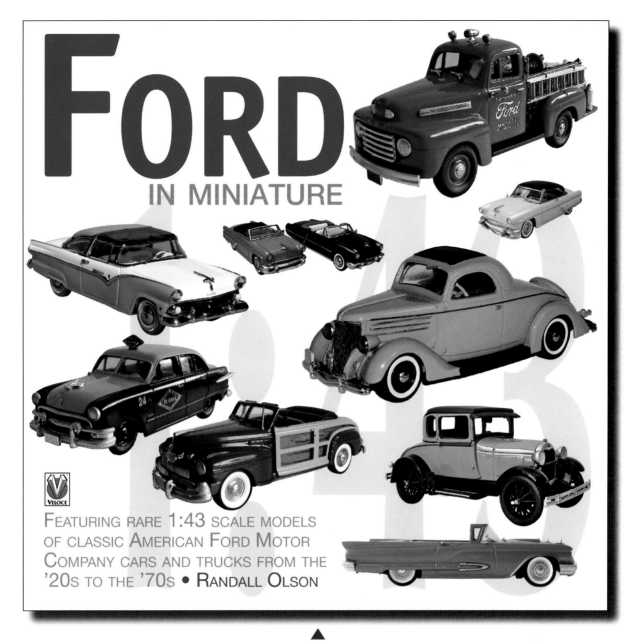

▲
Ford in Miniature by Randall Olson
Hardback • 25x25cm • £19.99 • 128 pages • 400 colour photos • ISBN: 978-1-84584-027-3 • UPC: 6-36847-04027-7

This colourful book captures some of the most beautiful and rare scale models ever made of American Ford, Edsel, Lincoln, and Mercury cars and light trucks from the classic 1930-69 period. These unusual and expensive models have flawless finishing and astounding detail: a *must* for scale model and Ford buffs.

During the last thirty years, a small number of builders have devoted themselves to making, by hand, model cars in scale. Often limited to only a few hundred pieces, these unusual and expensive models have flawless finishing and astounding detail.

For the first time ever in one source, the author has assembled hundreds of high-resolution colour photographs from his and others' private collections, and from the builders themselves. Read about the history of these Ford replicas, the cars they are modelled upon, and learn where you can get them.

MORE FROM VELOCE PUBLISHING:

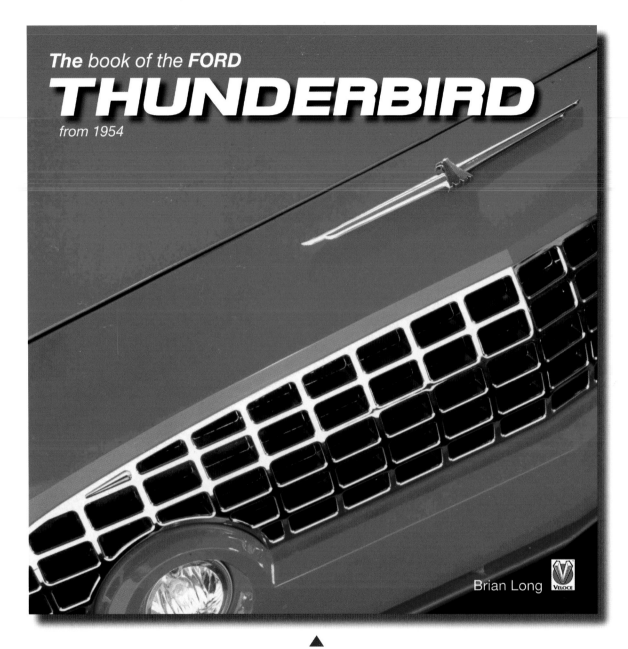

The book of the *FORD*

THUNDERBIRD

from 1954

Brian Long

▲

The Book of the Ford Thunderbird from 1954 by Brian Long
Hardback • 25x25cm • £40.00 • 288 pages • Over 500 photos • ISBN: 978-1-904788-47-8 • UPC: 6-36847-00347-0

The definitive history of the Ford Thunderbird. It's all here: from concept, through all yearly changes until the Thunderbird's demise in the 1990s and its rebirth in the new millennium, looking at the model's numerous competition exploits along the way.
The American automotive scene was changed forever when Ford launched its legendary 1955 Thunderbird. Half a century and innumerable facelifts later, the Thunderbird still manages to capture the heart of American car enthusiasts with its sporting character and bold styling. In addition, it is illustrated throughout with contemporary material to help those looking for originality. Written with full co-operation from Ford, this is a superbly comprehensive reference and a great story!

INDEX

www.velocebooks.com/www.veloce.co.uk
All current books • New book news • Special offers • Gift vouchers

▲

Citroën DS - Design Icon by Malcolm Bobbitt

Hardback • 25x20.7cm • £34.99 • 208 pages • 250 mainly colour pictures • ISBN: 978-1-904788-30-0 • UPC: 6-36847-00330-2

The most radical of Citroën's idiosyncratic offerings, the DS was sensational when introduced in 1955. Twenty years and 1.45 million cars later it was still technically advanced compared to most other cars. Revolutionary in driving characteristics and comfort, it remains one of the most innovative cars of all time and one of today's great classics.

MORE FROM VELOCE PUBLISHING:

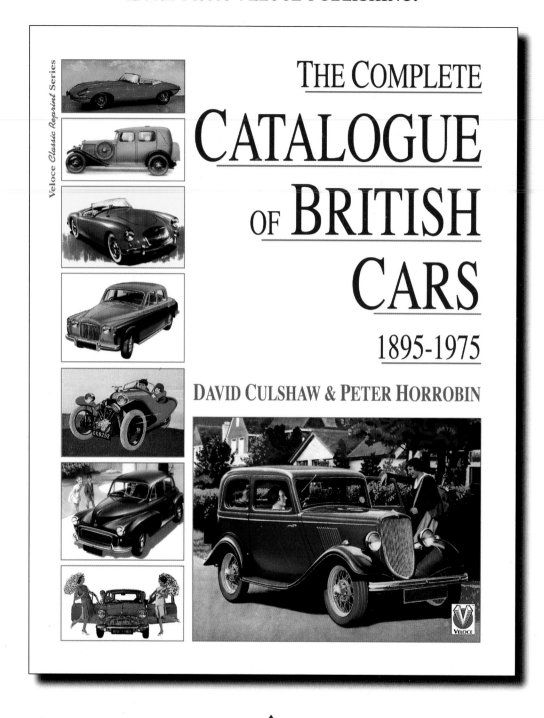

Veloce Classic Reprint Series

THE COMPLETE
CATALOGUE
OF BRITISH
CARS
1895-1975

DAVID CULSHAW & PETER HORROBIN

▲

The Complete Catalogue of British Cars 1895-1975 by David Culshaw & Peter Horrobin
Hardback • 28x21.5cm • £30.00 • 496 pages • More than 1000 photographs • ISBN: 978-1-874105-93-0 • UPC: 6-36847-00093-6

Available again! The famous "Culshaw & Horrobin". The most comprehensive account of British cars ever published in one volume, this book presents a huge amount of information – historical as well as technical – in a way which will serve the needs of the dedicated enthusiast, automotive historian and the general reader.